EXPLORING HUMAN PSYCHOLOGY

LEARNER'S PERSPECTIVE

DR. MUKTA GOYAL

Contents

Preface   *v*

List Of Authors   *vii*

1. Psychology: As A Scientific Study Of Behaviour   1

2. Learners' Psychology: The Improvement Of Learner Attitudes   10

3. Concept Of Education And Psychology   24

4. Growth And Development   29

5. Emotional Psychology: A Study Of Different Emotions   38

6. Personality Concepts And Theories   47

7. Dual Personality Of Dr. Jekyll   56

8. Behavioural Finance: Study Of The Impacts Of Psychology On   64
   Investors And Financial Markets

9. Concept Of Personality,types, Traits And Adjustment   72

10. Fostering Creativity At Workplace   82

11. Ivan Pavlov And His Discovery Of Classical Conditioning   90

12. A Spectrum Of Jungian Psychology In Jhumpa Lahiri's "   97
    Interpreter Of Maladies"

13. Freud's Psychoanalytic Theory On Personality   103

14. The Concept Of Intelligence: Useful Or Useless?   119

15. Understanding And Managing Disruptive Behavior In   129
    Adolescents

16. Cognitive And Moral Development In Learners   140

17. Adjustment Concept And Defence Mechanism   149

18. Bandura's Theory Of Social Learning   154

19. Creativity's Invention   161

Preface

The book "Exploring Human Psychology" has been introduced to provide current information and meet the urgent needs of students pursuing B.Ed, M.Ed, and B.A . An (Education) degree and preparing for NET-JRF, SET, SLET, and other competitive exams. We are confident that this book meets all essential requirements, and its widespread distribution will significantly impact educational theory. In completing this self-imposed stupendous task, the authors were acutely aware of their numerous limitations in light of the diverse subject-matter required to complete this volume. Human Psychology has been taught as a major subject in Teacher Education Programs at various levels on the implicit assumption that knowledge of Human Psychology provides insight into problems of teaching learning and develops other necessary professional skills and competencies in progressive teachers to face the classroom teaching give the teacher much of what he needs to achieve his goals by enabling him to understand, control, and predict the behaviour of his students. Psychologists frequently define learning as a relatively permanent change in behaviour as a result of experience. The psychology of learning is concerned with various issues concerning how people learn and interact with their surroundings. The behaviourists believed that psychology should be the scientific study of observable behaviour.

Our mindsets influence whether we seek out and persevere in the face of difficulties, whether we believe others should be given opportunities to learn, whether we become depressed, and even whether we act prejudiced. In a nutshell, mindsets matter. Successfully instilling a new mindset necessitates the careful application of persuasion principles.

This book assists students in organising their conceptual thinking about psychology. Psychological science has much to offer in terms of improving classroom teaching and learning. Teaching and learning are inextricably linked to cognitive, motivational, social interaction, and communication factors in human development.

Each chapter includes one or two features that connect the chapter's principles to real-world applications in business, the environment, health, law, learning, and other relevant domains.

Dr Mukta Goyal

List Of Authors

• • •

- *Kaniska Tomar, Pupil Teacher, Manvi Institute of Education and Technology, SCERT, Delhi.*
- *Mr. UdayModak ,Assistant Professor,Bhavan's Tripura College of Teacher Education, Bimangarh, Narasingarh, Agartala, Tripura.*
- *Dr Mukta Goyal, Principal, Manvi Institute of Education and Technology, SCERT, Delhi.*
- *Ms.Rashima Sharma, Asst. Professor, Trinity Institute of Professional Studies, Dwarka, New Delhi.*
- *Dr. Savita Mishra,Principal,Vidyasagar College of Education, Phansidewa, Darjeeling.*
- *Tanwangini Sahani, Student, MBA (FA), GGSIPU, Delhi.*
- *Swati Singh, Student, B.Voc. Software Development, Guru Nanak Dev. Institute of Technology, Delhi.*
- *Dr. D. SASI DEVI, Assistant Professor in English, PG & Research Department of English, Thiagarajar College, Affiliated to Madurai Kamaraj University, Madurai.*
- *Hardik Sawhney, Risk Analyst, Credit Suisse, Mumbai.*
- *Pranati das, Student, Meerabai Institute of Technology, Maharani Bagh, GGSIPU, Delhi.*
- *Dr.Archana Deshpande, Associate Professor, Guru Nanak Institute of Management, GGSIPU, Delhi.*
- *Dr.Anshika Rajvanshi, Assistant Professor, Department of Management, IIMT, Delhi.*
- *Muskan Jindal, BA(Hons) Psychology, MA Psychology.*
- *Dr I. Saranya, Assistant Professor of English & IQAC Staff Coordinator, PG & Research Department of English, Thiagarajar College,(Affiliated to Madurai Kamaraj University), Madurai.*
- *Gurpinder Kumar, Assistant Professor, Centre for Women's Studies, University of Allahabad, Prayagraj, UP-211002, INDIA.*
- *Dr. Ekata Gupta,Associate Professor,Guru Nanak Institute of management, Delhi.*
- *Kanishka Tomar, Pupil Teacher, Manvi Institute of Education and*

Technology, SCERT,DelhI.

- *Mr. K. C. Malik, Retired Associate Professor, Sri Venkateswara College, University of Delhi.*
- *Dr Abhishek Srivastava, Associate Professor, Faculty of Management Studies, Gopal Narayan Singh University, Rohtas, Bihar.*
- *Divine Tomar, Pupil Teacher, Manvi Institute of Education andTechnology, SCERT, Delhi.*
- *Mr.Anand Prakash Dube,Associate Professor, School of Management Sciences, Varanasi.*
- *Krittibas Datta,State Aided College Teacher,Department of Political Science,Jalangi Mahavidyalaya, Murshidabad,West Bengal, India.*

CHAPTER I

PSYCHOLOGY: AS A SCIENTIFIC STUDY OF BEHAVIOUR

Kaniska Tomar, Pupil Teacher, Manvi Institute of Education and Technology, SCERT, Delhi.
Mr. UdayModak ,Assistant Professor,Bhavan's Tripura College of Teacher Education,Bimangarh, Narasingarh, Agartala, Tripura.

• • •

Introduction

The scientific study of the mind and behaviour is called psychology. Psychologists are actively interested in researching and comprehending how the mind, the brain, and behaviour work. With close ties to the social sciences, medical sciences, and educational sciences, psychology is regarded as a "Hub Science" (Boyack, Klavans, & Borner, 2005).

One of the more fascinating and crucial ways of thinking and acting in cultures is science. Therefore, the empirical focus of psychologists should be on scientific thought and behaviour.

The academic and applied field of psychology deals with the rational investigation of thought and action. The term "psychology" also refers to the application of this knowledge to many aspects of human activity, such as how people live their daily lives and how to cure mental illnesses.

Because psychology aims to understand people's brain processes and behaviour, it varies from the other social sciences, such as anthropology, economics, political science, and sociology. Psychology is largely concerned with the connection of mental processes and behaviour on a systemic level, whereas biology and neuroscience investigate the biological or brain processes and how they relate to the subjective mental consequences they create. While biological psychology focuses on the biological underpinnings of behaviour and mental states, the discipline of neuropsychology analyses real brain processes.

The study of behaviour, the mind, and cognition, as well as the unconscious neural underpinnings of behaviour, are all covered by the academic and practical field of psychology. The term "psychology" also refers to the application of such knowledge to many aspects of human activity, such as the treatment of mental disease and issues that arise in people's daily lives. Although it primarily focuses on humans, psychology research can also include studies of animal behaviour and mental functioning, either as a separate field in and of itself (such as animal cognition and ethology) or, more controversially, as a means of comparison to better understand human psychology (including comparative psychology). The study of behaviour and mental processes is known as psychology.

All psychologists rely on scientific procedures, notwithstanding the variations in their specialisations, research areas, and methodology. While psychologist-practitioners including clinical, counselling, industrial-organizational, and school psychologists use existing research to improve people's daily lives, research psychologists employ scientific methods to generate new understanding about the causes of behaviour. Both academics and practitioners value the science of psychology.

Although a psychological viewpoint on scientific cognition and behaviour has existed for about 100 years, a formal field of science psychology has only recently started to take shape.

The goal of the psychology of science is to conduct an empirical investigation of the complete spectrum of psychological mechanisms underlying scientific behaviour, aptitude, and innovation. The field is undoubtedly young and has developed slowly in comparison to other scientific disciplines. The phrases philosophy of science, history of science, and sociology of science are generally understood by everyone. However, many others, including other psychologists, frequently have no idea what you mean when you discuss the "psychology of science."

The central claim of psychology of science is that the best theoretical and empirical tools at our disposal as psychologists must be used in order to fully appreciate and comprehend scientific thought and behaviour, from the infant trying to understand the world to the historically great scientific discoveries. In order to understand the mechanisms underlying scientific cognition and behaviour, psychology is ideally suited. But when I use the word "science," I'm not just referring to the beliefs and actions of actual scientists. Instead, children and adolescents can display implicit and developing scientific thought and behaviour, as well as explicit and developed thought and behaviour articulated by scientists (Feist, 2006; Proctor & Capaldi, 2012). The psychological factors influencing the thoughts and behaviours of professional scientists are only one aspect of science psychology. It also includes ideas like how people develop intellectually as children, adolescents, and adults; how high school kids are talented and interested in science; how college students lose interest in science; and even how adults think and believe in pseudoscience. In essence, everybody engaging in implicit or explicit scientific thought and behaviour is concerned by science psychology. There are as many scientific psychologies as there are significant subfields in psychology. This article must be brief, thus a comprehensive and integrated examination of the psychology of science as a whole is not possible (see Feist, 2006; Feist & Gorman, 2013; Gholson et al., 1989; Proctor & Capaldi, 2012; Simonton , 1988, for more detailed treatments). I will still make an effort to give the reader a thorough and accurate sample of the problems the field has addressed while also raising some potential new ones for future study by researchers on the psychological underpinnings of scientific cognition and behaviour. The psychology of science is still in its infancy, but it is similar to its parent field and may be broken down into similar subdisciplinary groups, including neuroscientific, cognitive, developmental, social, personality, educational, and clinical psychologies of science.

Brain-based psychology

Making sense of and organising sensory input is one of the brain's main jobs, along with controlling the body. At the risk of oversimplification, seeking to comprehend our experience of the physical, biological, and social worlds is also what science is about. A more methodical and explicit version of daily intuitive or implicit thought occurs in scientific thought (Feist, 2006; Proctor & Capaldi, 2012). Although it is a challenging endeavour, trying to comprehend the genetic and brain systems involved in scientific thought is the ideal area of study for the psychology of science. Real-time brain imaging for problem-solving and scientific reasoning is not simple or inexpensive to obtain. But lately, some psychologists have started looking at this, with Jonathan Fugelsang and Kevin Dunbar leading the charge. They have concentrated on the brain processes that underlie causal and scientific reasoning.

For instance, Fugelsang and Dunbar (2005) contend that when it comes to reasonable ideas, people are more attentive to the evidence than when it comes to improbable ones. They found that neuronal mechanisms in a region around the hippocampus, the brain's learning and memory centre, are active when data are congruent with one's theory. Brain mechanisms in the prefrontal cortex, areas involved in mistake detection, attentiveness, and monitoring opposing viewpoints, are active when data do not support one's theory (cf. Dunbar et al., 2007).

Insightful psychology

Cognitive psychology is arguably the most developed branch of science-based psychology among all other branches (Tweney, 1998). Psychologists have looked into how many cognitive processes, such as problem-solving, confirmation bias, creativity, analogical and metaphorical reasoning, visualising, and remembering, relate to scientific cognition. Scientists solving simulated difficulties and actual problems in the lab have all been studied by cognitive psychologists of science. They have also studied the thought processes of historical figures in science.

But during the past ten years, an increasing number of cognitive psychologists have entered laboratories to watch, document, and examine how scientists think and behave while working. This approach was invented by Kevin Dunbar. His key early discoveries included the utilisation of anomalies and unexpected outcomes as sources for new theories and experiments, as well as the significance of analogies in the development of hypotheses and the interpretation of findings (Dunbar, 2000). Others have pursued this line of inquiry and discovered similar results, such as the fact that applied scientists (meteorologists), for example, were more likely to mentally manipulate and spatially rotate the image, whereas pure scientists (astronomers and physicists), were more likely to run through a conceptual simulation (a "what if") of the unexpected result (Trickett et al., 2009).

Psychological development

Developmental psychologists tackle a variety of fascinating issues in scientific behaviour and mind, including: How do young toddlers and newborns form implicit ideas and notions about how the world functions, and are these theories and concepts unique in the physical, biological, and social spheres, for example? How does a person's interest in science grow? When do scientific creativity and production peaked? Does birth order affect how people become interested in and successful in science? Does a boy's or girl's interest in science develop differently throughout time?

I can only briefly discuss a few of the empirical discoveries that provide answers to some of these queries. According to recent studies (Gopnik, 2009; Xu & Garcia, 2008), babies as young as eight months old can understand probability, and kids as young as four years old may accurately deduce causal relationships from bar graphs (Koerber & Sodian, 2009).

Other developmental researchers have investigated how well children and teenagers can discriminate between their theories and the supporting data for those views, which is a crucial aspect of scientific thinking. Children, teenagers, and nonscientist adults typically evaluate explanations and evidence using different standards, are generally less adept at distinguishing between theory and evidence, and frequently use their own opinions as support for those beliefs (Brewer et al., 2000; Klahr, 2000; Kuhn & Pearsall, 2000). Researchers have discovered that believing information is definitive and absolute, that is, either right or wrong, is one cause for the inability to discern theory from fact (Yang & Tsai, 2010). Children are better equipped to understand that evidence is distinct from belief if they perceive knowledge as less absolute and certain. However, Koslowski (1996) offers convincing proof that humans are capable of more sophisticated scientific thinking than is occasionally suggested by other researchers.

Public policy

The study of social psychology focuses on how actual or hypothetical other individuals can affect a person's behaviour or thoughts. Social psychology is used to study how scientists persuade people to change their minds (attitudes), how scientific teams cooperate and compete with one another, how scientific leaders set rules that influence the creativity and productivity of scientific teams, and how partnerships develop to promote creative team productivity (Shadish & Fuller, 1994). Robert Rosenthal's revolutionary research on experimenter effects, or how the experimenter can genuinely influence participant behaviour and, consequently, study results in unconscious and unknowing ways, is one of the more fascinating applications of social psychology of science (Rosenthal, 1994). Other more recent social psychological studies of scientific behaviour have concentrated on the ways in which computer-based communication (email, texting, etc.) facilitates team collaborations in science (Aragon et al., 2009), the ways in which conflict and cooperation affect scientific creativity (Schultz & Seuffert, 2013), the ways in which leadership qualities affect creative output in scientific groups (Hemlin et al., 2004), and the ways in which different collaborative patterns and authorship bonds exist in different (Liberman & Wolf, 1998).

Personal characteristics

Certain behaviours are more and less likely based on personality attributes. The topic is whether particular patterns of personality qualities make scientific thought, performance, and action more likely. Yes, it is the answer.

Scientists are moderately more conscientious and less open to experience than nonscientists, according to the findings of a meta-analysis of 26 research reporting effect sizes on the relationship between personality and scientific curiosity (Feist, 1998).

Low openness is characterised by being traditional, socialised, and inflexible, whereas conscientiousness is characterised by being cautious, careful, fastidious, and self-controlled. Similar to this, a meta-analysis of 28 research comparing the personalities of creative and less creative scientists discovered that creative scientists differ from their less creative counterparts in that they are more self-assured, more open to new experiences, and less conscientious (Feist, 1998).

In essence, high conscientiousness and low openness are the personality traits that increase the likelihood of having an interest in science, whereas high openness, low conscientiousness, and high confidence increase the likelihood of having an interest in science.

By quantifying the extent of hereditary influence of personality on scientific achievement, Dean Simonton recently made strides in the field of personality psychology of science (Simonton, 2008). Simonton calculated the impact of genetic influences on scientific performance and achievement using effect sizes from meta-analytic and behavior-genetic studies of scientific talent. He discovered that between 37% and 48% of the projected variance in scientific talent was explained by the upper-bound estimates of genetic impacts.

Academic psychology

The state of mathematics and scientific education can be greatly improved with the help of psychological science. According to Newcombe and colleagues (2009), there are four main areas where psychology may and has contributed: early mathematical comprehension, understanding of science, social and motivational variables influencing interest in science and mathematics, and evaluating math and science learning. For instance, Zimmerman and Croker (2013) assert that learning scientific concepts and practises involves both cognitive and metacognitive skills. According to Eccles et al. (quoted in Newcombe et al., 2009), beliefs and success expectations have a significant impact on students' decisions to enrol in advanced mathematics and science courses. Other psychological factors that influence interest, performance, and achievement in math and scientific classes include self-efficacy, intrinsic motivation, and self-identity.

Applied psychology

The relationship between science and mental health is the subject of one of the least established but nonetheless most fascinating scientific psychology. The issue is whether scientists experience any more severe mental health issues than the general population. Indeed, throughout history, scientists such as Tesla, Faraday, and Newton have all been associated with some form of psychological disease.

We must first understand the baseline prevalence of mental health issues in the population in order to respond to this question. According to the most current survey, 46% of Americans will experience at least one diagnosable mental health episode over their lives (Kessler et al., 2005).

However, natural scientists are less prone to have mental illness than other creative groups (28 per cent vs. 59 per cent: Ludwig, 1995). Even social scientists had a slightly lower lifetime risk of experiencing one episode of psychological disturbance compared to other creative groups (51 per cent versus 59 per cent: Ludwig, 1995). Similar to how artists and musicians score higher on odd experiences and cognitive disorganisation than scientists do, recent self-report research utilising nonclinical assessments of schizotypy (i.e. eccentricity) supports the opposite (Rawlings & Locarnini, 2008). One could be tempted to draw the conclusion that scientists are less likely than other creative persons to experience mental health issues.

That may very well be the case, but we must first make a warning known: It's possible that science has a tendency to weed out people with mental health issues in a manner that art, music, and poetry do not. In other words, than aspiring artists, aspiring scientists with mental health issues will be less likely to be recruited or complete their degrees. Science calls for sustained concentration on an issue over an extended length of time, as well as frequent attendance in a lab or consistent problem-solving.

A person is less likely to succeed as a scientist if they are unable to work methodically and consistently.

Conclusions

There was no official science psychology discipline up to the middle of the 2000s. There is today, despite the fact that it is still mostly in its infancy and requires more methodical and integrated work. One overarching conclusion that can be drawn from this review is that there are numerous different areas of psychology, including neuroscience, cognition, development, educational psychology, personality, social psychology, and clinical psychology, that have significant bearing on how people become interested in science, how they reason about science, and how they end up becoming scientists and mathematicians. A psychological viewpoint is required to fully comprehend scientific curiosity, thought, talent, and achievement, which is the overall finding from these diverse fields of research.

Only the accumulated knowledge of all of science's psychologies can put the puzzle pieces of how scientists grow, mature, and achieve together. Undoubtedly, as much as anything else, the integration of all of these data calls for incisive and original theorising. Unified theorising is missing in the social sciences generally, and improving it is one of the field's top priorities going forward.

A greater knowledge of the research process will, in the end, encourage scientists to reflect more critically on their hypotheses and techniques, which will result in higher-quality research, which is one of the key applied goals of psychology of science.

In fact, the psychology of science has started to be used to inform scientific lab development and organisation, as well as science of science policy. Additionally, from a purely scientific standpoint, the knowledge of scientific thought, motivation, curiosity, creativity, social influence, mental disease, and personality has been lacking these significant empirical and theoretical contributions. Science is a driving force in contemporary society. If we are to comprehend this driving force and increase our gifted young people's interest in science and scientific careers, we must continue to use and build a sound and mature science psychology.

References

- https://www.taylorfrancis.com/books/mono/10.4324/9780203779408/scientific-study-social-behaviour-psychology-revivals-michael-argyle
- Psychology as the scientific study of behaviour can be found at this website: https://books.google.co.in/books?hl=en&lr=&id=PVQDAedulXcC&oi=fnd&pg=PR2&dq=Psychology as the Scientific Study of Behavior&ots=aYbBtdLGDr&sig=mkP3XiBxHIVwcroTL-4pDejD vA&re
- W. McDougall (1912). the study of behaviour, psychology (No. 41). H. Holt.

- Psychology is the scientific study of the functioning of the brain and behaviour, according to https://psychology.osu.edu/about/what-psychology#::text=Psychology.
- https://www.simplypsychology.org/whatispsychology.html
- https://en.wikibooks.org/wiki/Introduction to Psychology/ Introduction
- https://opentextbc.ca/introductiontopsychology/chapter/ 1-1-psychology-as-a-science/
- https://www.bps.org.uk/psychologist/psychology-scientific-thought-and-behaviour
- https://www.taylorfrancis.com/books/mono/10.4324/ 9780203779408/scientific-study-social-behaviour-psychology-revivals-michael-argyle

CHAPTER II

LEARNERS' PSYCHOLOGY: THE IMPROVEMENT OF LEARNER ATTITUDES

Dr Mukta Goyal, Principal, Manvi Institute of Education and Technology, SCERT, Delhi.

• • •

INTRODUCTION

Educational Psychology and consists of two words Psychology and Education. While Genral Psychology is a pure science. Educational Psychology is its application in the field of education with the aim of socializing man and modifying his behaviour. According to Crow and Crow Educational Psychology describes and explains the learning experiences of an individual from birth through old age. Skinner defines Educational Psychology as "that branch of Psychology which deals with teaching and learning" 2 Stephen – "Educational Psychology is the systematic study of the educational growth and development of a child." Judd – "Educational Psychology is the Science which explains the changes that take place in the individuals as they pass through the various stages of development." Peel- "Educational Psychology is the science of Education." Educational psychology is one of the branches of applies psychology concerned with the application of the principles, techniques and other resourse of psychology to the solution of the problems confronting the teacher attempting to direct the growth of children toward defined objectives.

More specifically, we can say educational psychology is concerned with an understanding of:

• The child, his development, his need and his potentialities.

• The learning situation including group dynamics as the affect learning.

• The learning process its nature and the ways to make it effective. Stated differently, the Central theme of Educational Psychology is the Psychology of learning.

PSYCHOLOGY OF LEARNING

This area is concerned with such problems as : How do children acquire skills? When is learning more effective? What are the factors that help the learning Process? How do we measure the amount of learning? Are there any economic methods of memorizing? Why do we forget? Can memory be improved? Dose the study of Sanskrit helps than study of Hindi? Psychology helps the teacher to get answers to these questions. It tells us that learning becomes more effective if factors like motivation and interest are taken into consideration by every teacher. The knowledge of psychology has helped the teacher in modifying her approach to the teaching-learning process. The study of educational Psychology has brought about change in the approach and therefore we have child centred education. Psychological principles are used in the formulation of curriculum for a different stage. Attempts are made to provide subjects and activities in the curriculum which are in conformity with the needs of the students, their developmental characteristics, learning patterns and also needs of the society.

Psychologists frequently define learning as a relatively permanent change in behaviour as a result of experience. The psychology of learning is concerned with various issues concerning how people learn and interact with their surroundings.

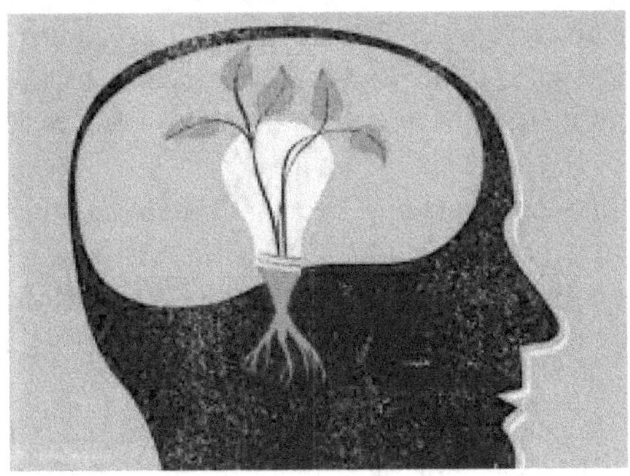

psychologycompass.com

John B. Watson, a psychologist, was one of the first to investigate how learning influences behaviour, proposing that all behaviours are the result of the learning process. Watson's work gave rise to a school of thought known as behaviourism. The behavioural school of thought proposed studying internal thoughts, memories, and other subjective mental processes.

The behaviourists believed that psychology should be the scientific study of observable behaviour. During the first half of the twentieth century, behaviourism flourished and made significant contributions to our understanding.

It is fact that psychology deals with attitude and characters of learners in learning process. In learning process, it is mandatory for the teacher to know about the learners' personality and his family background for fruitful results from learners in the learning process.

Learning of the environment plays a significant role in brain development. As, adolescent performs an important mental task. The neural network that supports those abilities strengthen necessary their cognitive, emotion-regulate a memory skills. Without opportunities to use these skills, these networks remain under-developed making it challenging for individuals to engage in higher order thinker as adults. [i] (Robyn Harper, August 2018)

There are different types of psychologies but social psychology is that psychology which studies the behavior of mankind. But the requirements of body and soul are different while every man is compound of soul and body. The soul is invisible while body is visible. In societies, there are active and popular organizations on the basis characters of their members or employees or combination of management and members also.[ii] (Masood Tahira Dr., 2017)

Anyhow, behind any person's behavior, there are many factors that influence particular person to adopt strict or soft corner in behavior. In this, past incidents of his life, past accidents of relatives or friends and his current financial position and current friend or relatives attitudes to this particular are also.

As author of 'Social Psychology', stated that behind person's attitudes, past events effect his behavior regarding present thing.[iii] (Mughal Tariq Mahmood, 2013) In the present world, fact is that if any person is deceived by some other person of any other particular tribe or of particular department, definitely, his behavior will be bitter in future on the bases of past events about persons of this particular tribe or department. Similarly, if any learner gets good guidance and feels impressive from any institution, definitely in future, that particular person will have positive views and guides other to get admission in this institution as proposal.

Similarly, in the changing of persons' behaviors, current incidents or losses make persons bitter regarding behavior of the people of societies. [iv]

(Mughal Tariq Mahmood, 2013) In societies, if you want spread positive activities then it is necessary that positive values must be encouraged and the persons who are uncivilized, these must be discouraged and their weaknesses must be pinpointed for correction not for discussion.

In educational institutions, generally, teachers' attitudes toward hard-working students and intelligent students remain positive and most teachers appreciate these types of learners due to their efficacy in studies. Similarly in any organization, hardworking and efficient workers will be encouraged in the eyes of their boss. Therefore, in educational institutions, such types of steps must be taken so that teachers could involve students in teaching activities. In this way, students can become hard working and civilized if regular care is done.

In the learning process in schools, the teacher's behavior toward the students who complete their work, will be good and favorable rather than those who do not do homework or are dull in-class activities. [v] (Bhutta Waqar Ahmad, 2009) It is the duty of teachers they should not to neglect the dull students in learning activities so that they can improve their educational weaknesses. It is my practical experience that with proper care, dull and weak students are improved with the passage of time. While if these are neglected and not provided proper care, they leave their studies an early age.

Furthermore, if someone wants to change person's behaviors then by creating a difficult situation about the future or the danger of foreign attacks, changing in behavior of the people may occur.[vi] (Mansoor Ali Akbar, 1998) As in the perceptions of war, or danger of war, most people will increase shopping than demand due to the danger of war. Similarly, if educated persons are employed on heavy earnings, this will be encouragement for the present learners to study more on the hope of good paying jobs. If educated persons remain unemployed or can gain a low level of income. This will be actually discouraging for present learners so that they will continue studying without any interest.

Anyhow, some scholars opine that teachers can correct the behaviors of their students' attitudes if they are not doing well. While some others opine that teachers cannot correct students' attitudes because they favor of the given quotation, 'Nature cannot change.' Anyhow, changing of students' attitude may be improved in some students while in some students, teachers' guidance may not be improved but for very low numbers, this may have occurred.

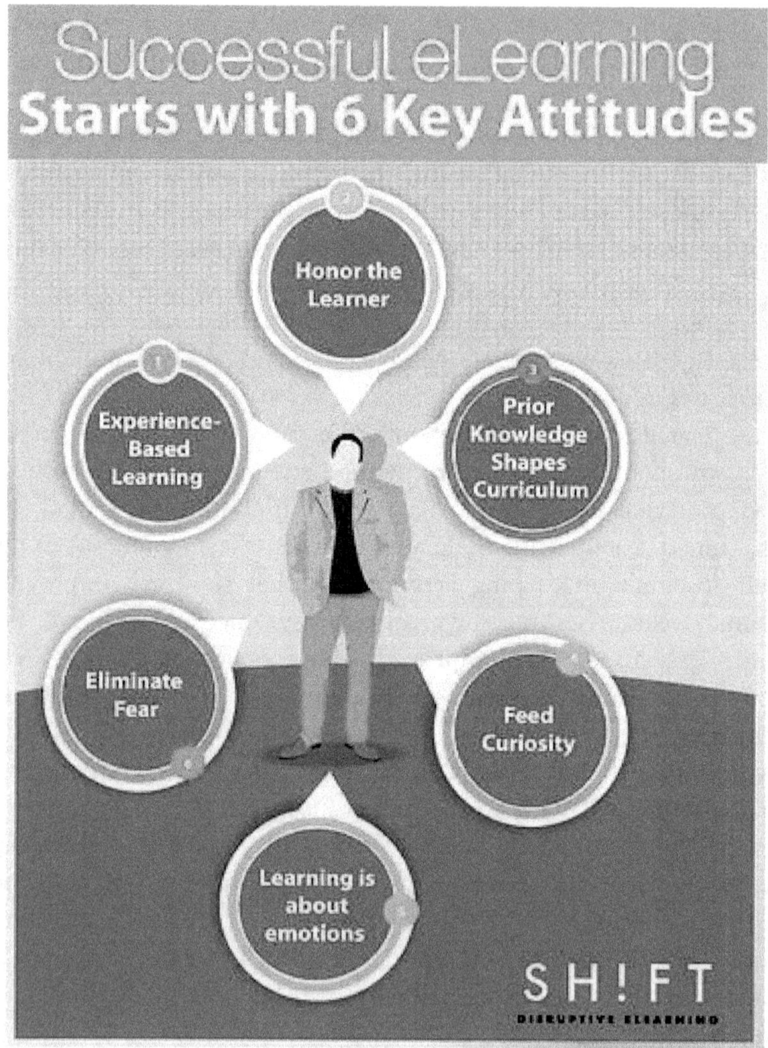

shiftelearning.com

Teachers cannot actually control their students' behavior. That's because the only behavior, person can control in his or her own. And when teachers try directly to restrict what say or do, they are usually left feelings frustrated and helpless. [vii] (Shari Gent, March 22, 2021)

Training of individuals is crucial for the promotion of civilized society. In actual, training of individuals in the present time will show its results/

outcomes in future. This is why, in every department of any country, training is provided for its employees so that a particular sense might be developed.

As, Allama Asad wrote that, societies can be built only in a result of training and the polite behaviors of trainers which are used in learning manners. [viii] (Muhammad Asad Allama, March 2009) learners' attitudes may be affected from the attitude of teachers or master trainers in learning or training activities. Similarly, if teacher's behavior is impressive then learners will be attracted from his style.

Similarly, if teacher will use rude behavior in teaching or in learning activities, this will be dangerous for students and students will feel boredom. Therefore, the learning process must be as so that learners feel happy in the learning process.

And teachers can control the wrong activities of students in class by presenting such style and manner so that concerning involved student try to avoid from wrong behavior or unsuitable behavior.[ix] (Shari Gent, March 22, 2021) Besides these, if wrong behavior is not corrected by the teacher, or if teachers continue teaching activities and students remain busy in their wrong activities in class, This means both groups are just spending their time, or it may be stated that time is being killed. Therefore, it is better for fruitful results in learning for the students and for the teachers that both should take interest fully. And teachers should perform their duties having fear of God with honestly. Same is upon for learners otherwise there is a need to change students' attitudes regarding learning.

While Edward Kang stated that, teachers can guide students to avoid ineffective studying habits in favor of ones that will increase their learning outcomes. Too often people imagine that long hours of studying are the best path to being a model straight a student. Yet research shows that highly successful students actually spend less time studying than their peers' do-they just study more effectively. [x] (Edward Kang, April 4, 2019)

As concerned the responsibility of teachers or learners concerned, this may be stated that children are innocent so they influence by things and people at once. Therefore, teachers and parents are more responsible as they know the time, the people, about good or bad values and attitudes of the people with their effects. This may support from Meaning of the Holy Prophet's sayings that every child takes his birth in nature but it is upon his parents that make him, a Muslim, Jew, Christian or follower of any other religion. The reason is that children are innocent so elders, the old and others are responsible to keep the children on track of success.

And **Emma Chippa** stated that students are just like agriculture and plants, as you will care the plants safe from any kinds of raw roots or grass, then they will be grow safely otherwise, there will be problems to grow safely and becoming civilized[xi]. (Emma Chiappetta, June 18, 2021)

It is empirical evidence that sometimes, educated parents cannot provide better guidance and better learning institution but sometimes uneducated persons can provide better guidance and a learning environment. Due to this, the children/learners of uneducated persons can achieve good marks and good values in the societies. This also refers that theoretical values are different from practical values. And for attaining good and civilized values/ manners, the adoption of practical values will be useful.

While **Edward Kang** stated that there are the following recommended techniques for high-intensity study habits. These are as under:

1. Pre-test;
2. Spaced practice;
3. Self-Quizzing;
4. Inter-learning practice;
5. Paraphrasing & Reflecting.[xii] (Edward Kang, April 4, 2019)

For fruitful learning and better techniques, the learner must involve himself in studying activities. And for preparation of any test, the learner must analyze himself by self-test before taking any test so that he can remove mistakes and shortcomings before the actual test time. The advantage of pre-test activities will be useful as it will provide a chance to paraphrase the sentences.

In Amin's view, habits become nature when actions are repeated again and again.[xiii] (Muhammad Amin Dr., 2004). In classes, it is duty of teachers and in homes; it is duty of parents that they must know about the actions of their young ones so that proper solutions for these actions must be proposed.

Without considering this, this habit is useful or not useful, or this habit is good for individuals or for societies. In learning institutions, it is the duty of teacher and management of institutions to provide better conditions for learning activities so that learners can adopt positive and cultured values.

The fact is that sociologists opine that the purpose of social and welfare organizations is to provide satisfaction to humanity regarding their needs. Therefore, mostly organizations are established especially for the promotion of the availability of basic needs without considering, caste, creed and color. [xiv] (Bhutta Waqar Ahmad, 2009)

3 main types of behavioral learning

According to the behavioral learning theory, objective observation best suits behavior. It usually involves the following concepts:

1. Classical conditioning

Classical conditioning describes the process of learning through association by linking a stimulus to a response. Physiologist Ivan Pavlov discovered the concept and studied it extensively. He first used a dog as his subject before later involving children in his work.

For example, Pavlov tested classical conditioning in his famous experiments with dogs. Before training began, Pavlov established that the dog salivated at the sight of food because it knew it was going to eat soon. He then introduced a bell as a neutral stimulus. The dog made no connection between the bell and the food. Pavlov conditioned the dog by ringing the bell and then giving it food. Eventually, the dog understood that the ringing bell meant it would receive food soon, so it salivated each time Pavlov rang the bell. Classical conditioning comprises four elements:

Unconditioned stimulus: An unconditioned stimulus triggers a response naturally. In Pavlov's exercise, the food is an unconditioned stimulus because it caused the dog to salivate.

Conditioned stimulus: A conditioned stimulus pairs with the unconditioned stimulus to trigger the same response. For example, Pavlov used the bell as the conditioned stimulus to cause the dog to salivate.

Unconditioned response: An unconditioned response occurs naturally as a reaction to the unconditioned stimulus. For instance, the dog's salivation to food was natural because it did so with no prompting from Pavlov.

Conditioned response: A conditioned response, such as the dog's salivation when the bell rings, occurs when a previously neutral stimulus creates an automatic response. Conditioned responses require training in classical conditioning.

2. Operant conditioning

The idea of operant conditioning was first studied by psychologist Edward Thorndike and later expanded and developed by psychologist B.F. Skinner. The theory states that the consequences of our previous actions determine how we choose behaviors. If a person does something that leads to punishment, they're less likely to repeat it. If their behavior results in an award, they're likely to do it again. Because of its association between behaviors and consequences, operant conditioning has two key concepts:

Reinforcement

Reinforcement learning refers to an event that increases the frequency of the behavior that follows it. This can be negative or positive, as both uses increase the behavior. Using reinforcement schedules, which define when and how often operant conditioning occurs, researchers and educators can determine how quickly and efficiently a person learns the new behavior. In positive reinforcement situations, the person receives a reward for specific behavior. In negative reinforcement situations, a person's behavior leads to the removal of an adverse event.

Example: Suzie realizes that when she smiles at her baby, her baby smiles back. She enjoys the consequence of her action, so she continues to do it. The baby's smile is a positive reinforcer. Suzie also knows that when her baby needs a diaper change, he cries. Suzie always changes the baby's diaper right away to stop the crying. The baby's crying is a negative reinforcer.

Punishment

Punishment is the other key concept of operant conditioning. Both positive and negative punishments impact behavior by decreasing the behavior associated with its consequence. Positive punishment is something a person receives that leads to a negative result, while negative punishment involves taking something away after an unfavorable behavior occurs.

Example: If a student forgets to study for a test and received a poor grade as a result, they are likely to remember to study the next time they have a test. Because their forgetfulness to study decreases, f they experience positive punishment. If the student's parents take away their gaming console because of a poor test grade, they experienced negative punishment, because the removal of something favorable prevents the behavior from occurring again.

3. Observational learning

Observational learning occurs when a person learns a behavior by seeing others do it. This method of learning shows that people can internalize information from their external environments and develop new habits based on observations. When a person watches the way other people react to an unfamiliar situation, they typically respond to the event in the same way. These instances eliminate the need for conditioning.

7 Practical Tips on How to Develop a Positive Attitude in Students

We know for a fact that positive thinking is good for our physical, mental, and emotional health. Consider these strategies to inspire a positive attitude and teach your virtual school student how to think positively this year and beyond:

1. Be an example.

Model a positive, encouraging attitude in all that you say, do, and believe. Optimism is contagious. Positive thinking tends to breed positive outcomes, and if your child sees positive outcomes from your attitude, he or she is more likely to want to experience the same positive outcomes. Show how optimism creates an ideal environment for happiness and how positivity influences the probability of success for any goal you may have. Sometimes seeing is believing, and there's no better place for your child to see it than within you.

2. Create a positive learning space for your student.

What better way to inspire optimism than establishing a hopeful environment? As you create a home school classroom bulletin board or planner, or decorate your child's online school workspace, post several positive quotes to keep motivation high. Here are some optimistic quotes for students. Maybe make it fun and turn your favorite positive quotes into kitchen fridge magnets. A positive environment can do wonders for eliminating negative thinking and encouraging healthy thoughts as your student tackles new learning challenges and opportunities.

3. Help your student visualize positive outcomes for all scenarios.

It's important to regularly plan goals with your student, and when doing so, clearly set the stage for what success looks like. How will it feel to accomplish the goal? What will the reward be? What does it mean to be successful? And why does it matter? Answering all of these questions can get your student excited about working toward the goal and will remind him or her of the positive outcomes to look forward to.

4. Eliminate negative talk.

When you hear your student say, "I can't do it," take a step back. Bring this negative attitude to your child's attention. Dive deeper into the meaning behind it. Ask questions:

"Why can't you do it?"

"What's holding you back?"

"How can I help?"

"What do you need to be able to do it?"

From there, lay out a plan to remove those barriers. Show your child that you are in this together, and together you can come up with a plan to turn "I can't" into "We can."

Additionally, volunteering or giving to someone in similar or more dire circumstances than yourself can have an impact on reversing negative attitudes into positive ones. Sometimes all that is needed is a shift in perspective.

Find volunteer opportunities for kids of all ages, and help your student see past their challenges.

5. Help your student change negative thinking patterns.

As you bring your child's negative words and thoughts to their attention, make sure you're encouraging him or her to replace the negative attitude with a positive one. This is a form of cognitive behavioral therapy, which is designed to change people's thinking or behavioral patterns that are linked to certain difficulties. In this case, the concept is simple: when you have a negative thought or reaction, notice it and replace it with a positive response. The more your student does this, the more positive their thoughts, words, and actions will be.

6. Be your student's biggest fan.

As an online school parent or Learning Coach, your attitude has a big influence on your child's self-confidence. Your belief in your student can help them learn to feel confident and self-accepting. Consider trying some of these self-acceptance activities to make your child aware of his or her unique strengths and weaknesses. In turn, your home school student can begin thinking positively, developing self-esteem, and embracing his or her identity.

7. Set up a rewards system that encourages positivity.

It's not unusual for children to lack motivation to be positive, especially when they're dealing with a defeat or a sense of failure. Setbacks are a part of life, but how do you teach a child to keep their chin up when things are going badly? The answer may be a rewards system that provides positive reinforcement for optimism. Follow these steps to implement a rewards system for your youngster.

Being positive 24/7 is difficult for most people, but that doesn't mean we can't try harder to maintain an optimistic attitude.

CONCLUSION

In nutshell, it may be stated that learning activities must be impressive for the learners so that it may guide dull and weak learners separately with special care. In learning activities, teachers' role or role of master trainer cannot be ignored. Furthermore, learners' role and their attitude may be changed if some are not taking interest in learning activities. Teachers and the mater trainers also keep in mind that their attitude also must be for the betterment of learners rather than not just for spending time. No doubt, learners' and trainers' attitude regarding values and manners must be ideal otherwise All these activities and trainer's words will not be fruitful for leaners if he is offering words only from mouth rather than core of hearts. Anyhow, with worldly education, religious education must be provided to the learners of particular religion that will create emotions to help humanity. Any teachers/ trainers must keep in mind, the sociological status and economic condition of learners so that they could behave them in light of condition which will be useful in learning process.

"Change your thoughts and you change your world."—Norman Vincent Peale, author of The Power of Positive Thinking

Negative thinking is like a giant wall. It closes you in, keeps you from accomplishing goals, and stops you from moving forward in life—whether you're trying to learn, grow, or just be happy.

A negative attitude will also hold a student back from his or her true potential. What's one way to stop this from happening? By encouraging a positive attitude. Having a positive attitude often leads to positive outcomes. Parents can play a huge role in teaching their school-age children how to think positively. In turn, those parents can have front-row seats for the amazing transformations that happen when k-12 students simply begin to believe in themselves.

References

[i] Robyn Harper (August 2018), "Science of adolescent affect students learning : How body & brain development affect student learning," retrieved from www.allyed.org, Washington: Alliance for excellent Education, p-1,

[ii] Masood Tahira Dr., (2017) "Why advice is ineffective", Lahore: Monthly periodical Turjuman-ul-quran, p-90.

[iii] Mughal Tariq Mahmood, (2013) " Social Psychology', Lahore: Urdu Science Board, p-206.

[iv] Mughal Tariq Mahmood,(2013) " Social Psychology', Lahore: Urdu Science Board, pp-218-221.

[v] Bhutta Waqar Ahmad," (2009). "Social Work", Lahore: Advanced Publishers, pp-66-67.

[vi] Mansoor Ali Akbar (1998) "Muslim Psychology", Lahore: Feroze Sons,pp-100-1-1.

[vii] Shari Gent, (March 22, 2021) "12 strategies to inspire listening learning and self-control", derived from www. additudemag.com, derived on 16Th July, 2021,p-1.

[viii] Muhammad Asad Allama, (March 2009) " importance of Sunnah", Lahore: Turjuman-ul-Quran, pp-33-34.

[ix] Shari Gent, (March 22, 2021) "12 strategies to inspire listening, learning and self-control", derived from www. additudemag.com, derived on 16Th July, 2021,pp-2-16.

[x] Edward Kang (April 4, 2019)" Research backed studying techniques, derived from www.edutopia.org, derived on 15th July, 2021, p-1.

[xi] Emma Chiappetta (June 18, 2021) "Cultivating Number sense among middle &high school students", derived from www.edutopia.org, pp-1-5.

[xii] Edward Kang (April 4, 2019)" Research backed studying techniques, derived from www.edutopia.org, derived on 15th July, 2021, pp-1-5.

[xiii] Muhammad Amin Dr., (2004) "Islam aor Tazkiya Nafs", Lahore: Urdu Science Board, pp-607-608.

[xiv] Bhutta Waqar Ahmad," (2009). "Social Work", Lahore: Advanced Publishers, pp-64-66.

[xv] Editor, (1988) " A comprehensive report on Madaris' efficacy" Islamabad: Ministry of religious affairs, pp-8-9.

[xvi] Rehman Khalid (2010) " Deeni Madaris, conditions, prospects and problems", Islamabad: Institute of policy studies, pp-17-19.

[xvii] Khalid saleem Mansoor (2003) "Deeni Madaris mey taleem", Islamabad: Institute of policy studies, pp-30-37.

[xviii] Shahab Qudratullah (2004) "Shahab Nama", Lahore: Sang-e- Meel Publications, pp-230- 240.

[xix] Monique Verhoeven, Astrid Mita poortuis & Monique Volman (March, 2019), " The role of schools in adolescents identity development, A literature Review, Educational Psychology Review Journal, Vol. 31, issue1, pp-1-2.

- https://www.indeed.com/career-advice/career-development/ psychology-of-learning

- https://archive.mu.ac.in/myweb_test/SYBA%20Study%20Material/edu-II%20psycho.pdf
- https://www.connectionsacademy.com/support/resources/article/7-tips-to-encourage-a-positive-attitude-in-students/

CHAPTER III

CONCEPT OF EDUCATION AND PSYCHOLOGY

Ms.Rashima Sharma, Asst. Professor, Trinity Institute of Professional Studies, Dwarka, New Delhi.

• • •

Introduction

The biological and societal components of human life are intertwined. While nourishment and reproduction maintain and transmit the biological part of human existence, education maintains and transmits the social aspect of human life. Because of his educable abilities, man stands out among the lower animals. He is gifted with brains, and he desires to stay active, vibrant, and even unique. The list of human accomplishments is extensive. How has all of this been accomplished? Via means of education when viewed from various angles, the concept of education resembles a diamond that appears to be of varied colours (nature) (point of view or philosophy of life).

The complex character of the human personality

- Complex nature of surroundings

- Different philosophies of life

- Different educational theories and practices are the reasons for different interpretations/definitions of education.

"The fate of India is currently being moulded in her classrooms," the Education Commission (1964-66) began its report with these lines. "The country has reached a stage in its economic and technological growth where a considerable effort must be made to reap the greatest value from the assets already developed and to ensure that the rewards of change reach all sectors," the NPE (1986) continued. Vidya / Knowledge / Learning / Education was regarded the 'third eye' of man by ancient Indian thinkers, as it gave him insight into all situations and taught him how to act; it led to our redemption in the mundane domain, as well as all-round advancement and wealth.

Meaning of education:

Education is the discipline concerned with methods of teaching and learning in schools or school-like settings, as opposed to various nonformal and informal socialisation methods.

Education is a discipline concerned with methods of teaching and learning in schools or school-like settings, as opposed to various nonformal and informal socialisation methods (e.g., rural development projects and education through parent-child relationships).

Education can be defined as the transmission of a society's values and accumulated knowledge. In this sense, it corresponds to what social scientists refer to as socialisation or enculturation.

Children are born without culture, whether they are conceived among New Guinea tribespeople, Renaissance Florentines, or Manhattan's middle classes. Education is intended to help them learn a culture, shape their behaviour in adulthood, and direct them toward their eventual role in society. In the most primitive cultures, there is often little formal learning—nothing resembling school, classes, or teachers. Instead, the entire environment and all activities are frequently viewed as school and classes, with many, if not all, adults acting as teachers. However, as societies become more complex, the amount of knowledge to be passed down from one generation to the next becomes greater than any one person can know, necessitating the development of more selective and selective methods of transmission.

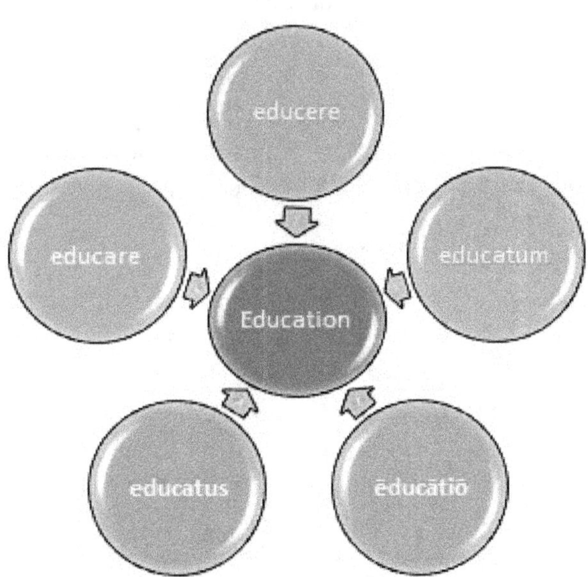

shikshatattwo.com

Psychology

Previously, psychology was considered a sub-discipline of philosophy. Psychology emerged as a separate scientific discipline when late-nineteenth-century physiologists began to examine the mind and how it functions using scientific methods.

Meaning of Psychology

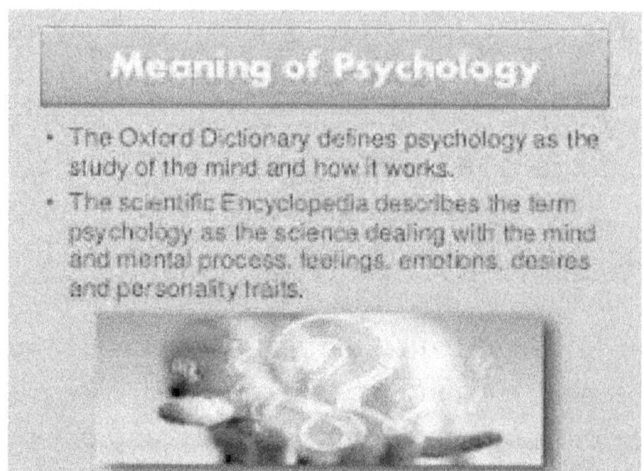

slideshare.net

In other words: Psychology is a combination of two words **psych** means **soul** and **logos** means **science**. During the development of psychology, it go through different meanings like the science of the soul, the science of mind, the science of consciousness and the science of behaviour.

Educational Psychology

The study of how individuals learn, including teaching methods, instructional processes, and individual differences in learning, is referred to as educational psychology. The idea is to figure out how people pick up new information and retain it.

This discipline of psychology encompasses not just the early childhood and adolescent learning processes, but also the social, emotional, and cognitive processes that are involved in learning throughout one's life.

Educational psychology encompasses a variety of fields such as developmental psychology, behavioural psychology, and cognitive psychology

Scope Of Educational Psychology

Relationship Between Education And Psychology

(1) **Psychological and educational goals:** Educational goals can be fixed with the help of a child's psychological changes. As a result, the markers for organizing any educational activity are needs, interest, aptitude, and attitude.

(2) **Psychology and curriculum:** When developing and preparing a curriculum, it is important to consider the child's developmental rate. As a result, they are complementary in the educational process.

(3) **Psychology and methods of teaching:** A teacher must offer instructions using a variety of approaches that are linked to the child's psychological problems, needs, and development.

(4) **Psychology and evaluation:** The evaluation and examination procedure as a whole should be based on psychological principles. Questions should be prepared with the children's typical development in mind. The following methods can help:

- Evaluation of child IQ (Intelligence test).
- Evaluate the factor of slow learning in the classroom situation.
- Attitude and scale of intelligence test.
- The Stanford- Binet scale of intelligence test.

The Stanford-Binet intelligence scale is a standardized test that assesses intelligence and cognitive abilities in children and adults aged two to twenty-three years, determining the presence of a learning disability or a developmental delay.

(5) **Psychology and discipline:** Discipline issues can be addressed with the use of appropriate psychological treatments. It also aids in the detection of many behavioural issues in children.

(6) **Administration and psychology:** The administrative process should be founded on psychological techniques. Individual variances should be taken into consideration when administering.

(7) **Psychology and the teacher:** To deal with a complex educational environment, a teacher should be a master of psychology. Teaching is an art, so he should be familiar with many psychological strategies in order to solve various children's problems.

(8) **Psychology and timetables, textbook preparation:** Curriculum workers, teachers, and administrators design appropriate timetables based on the learners' interests, time, suitability, and local circumstances.

Similarly, when preparing textbooks, he must consider the importance of the learner's psychological requirements, capacities, and development.

(9) **Educational Psychology and Several Phases of Growth:** An individual's personality and mental ability can be separated into different stages based on their growth, such as childhood, adolescence, and adulthood. Mental maturity is at various stages during these periods. Psychologists believe that if the reaching process is broken down into three parts, it will be much easier to learn. At different phases, different teaching methods are used. Without a thorough understanding of psychology, this is impossible.

(10) **Educational Psychology and Personality Development:** The goal of education is to help people develop their personalities. It is impossible to analyse the stimuli and responses of personality flaws, as well as their causes and reforms, without a thorough understanding of psychology.

Conclusion

As a result, psychology and education have a strong relationship. Psychologies education, according to Pestalozzi. Before beginning to teach, every teacher should study child psychology.

References

- https://research-education-edu.blogspot.com
- https://www.preservearticles.com
- **https://www.verywellmind.com**
- **www.sfu.**
- **https://www.cukashmir.ac.in**
- www.jaypeedigital.com
- **https://www.cukashmir.ac.in/**
- **https://www.cukashmir.ac.in**

CHAPTER IV

GROWTH AND DEVELOPMENT

Dr. Savita Mishra,Principal,Vidyasagar College of Education,Phansidewa, Darjeeling.

• • •

Introduction

The term growth implies on addition or increase in the bodily aspects that can be measured, for example, height, weight, size, muscles and length. It is best on biological processes that naturally occur over a period of time and relatively not or less influenced by context except for extreme illness or undernourishment. It eventually stops when the body parts reach the peak of their growth. While growth refers to the physical charges that an individual undergoes, development refers to certain charges that occur conception till death. It not only involves growth, but also entails disintegration and eventually decay. However, not all changes are considered as development. Rather, it applies to those changes that appear in orderly ways and are considerably permanent.

Principles of Growth and Development

Growth and development are inseparable but they different from each other. The growth represents the physical changes of an individual and development represents the overall changes, structure and shape of an individual. Knowledge of the growth and development at the various stage is very essential for the teacher. The teacher has to stimulate the growth and development of a child. He can do it only if he has proper knowledge of the growth and development at various stage.

- **Principle of Continuity:**

Development follows the principle of Continuity which means that **development is a continuous process. It starts with pre-natal and ends with death.**

- **Principle of Integration:**

Development thus involves a movement from the whole to parts and from parts to the whole and this way it is the integration of the whole and its parts as well as the specific and general responses. It enables a child to develop satisfactorily in relation to various aspects or dimension of his personality.

Example: Child first starts to learn hand movement finger movement and then learn the movement of both hand and finger together this is called integration.

- **Principle of lack of uniformity in the Developmental rate:**

Development through the continuous process, but does not exhibit steadiness and uniformity in terms of the rate of development in various development of personality or in the developmental periods and stage of life.

Example: A person may have a high rate of growth and development in term of height and weight but may not have the same pace of mental and social development.

- **Principle of Individual difference:**

Every organism is a distinct creation in itself. One of the most important principals of development is that involves individual differences. There is no fixed rate of development. That all children will learn to walk is universal, but the time at which each child takes his her first step may vary.

- **Principle of uniformity pattern:**

Although develop does not proceed at a uniform rate and shows marked individual differences with regard to the process and outcome of various stages of development, yet it follows a definite pattern in one or the other dimension which is uniform and universal with respect to the individual of a species.

- **Principle of proceeding from general to specific:**

While developing in relation to any aspect of personality. **The child first pickup or exhibit general response and learn how to show specific and**

goal – directed responses afterwards.

- **Principle of interaction between Heredity and Environment:**

Development of a child is a process that cannot be defined wholly based on either on **heredity**
Or environment. Both have to play an important role in development. There are arguments in favour of both. However, most of the psychologist agree that an interplay these two factors leads to development.

Where heredity decides or set some limits on development (mostly physical), environmental influences complete the developmental process (qualitative). Environmental influences provide space for multidimensional development through interaction with family, peers, society and so on. **Growth and development is a joint product of heredity and environment.**

- **Principle of interrelation:**

Various aspects or dimension of one's growth and development are interrelated. What is achieved or not achieved in on or other dimension in the course of the gradual and continuous process of the development surely affects the development of other dimensions?

A healthy body tends to develop a healthy mind and an emotionally stable, physically strong and socially conscious personality. Inadequate physical or mental development may, on the other hand, result in a socially or emotionally maladjusted personality.

- **Principle of Cephalocaudal:**

Development proceeds in the direction of the longitudinal axis.**Development from head to foot or toe.** That is why, before it becomes able to stand, the child first gains control over his head and arms and then on his legs.

- **Principle of proximodistal:**

Development of motor skills to Start at **Central body parts to outwards.** That is why, in the beginning, the child is seen to exercise control over the large fundamental muscles of the arm and then hand and only afterwards over the smaller of the fingers.

- **Principle of predictability:**

Development is predictable, which means that with the help of the uniformity of pattern and sequence of development. We can go to a great extent, forecast the general nature and behaviour of a child in one or more aspects or dimension at any particular stage of it's growth and development. We can know the particular age at which children will learn to walk, speak and so on.

- **Principle of Spiral versus Linear advancement:**

The child doesn't proceed straight or linear on the path of development at any stage never takes place with a constant or steady pace. After the child had developed to a certain level, there is likely to be a period of rest for consolidation of the developmental progress achieved till then. In advancing further, therefore, the development turn back and then moves forward again in a **spiral pattern.**

- **Principle of Association of Maturation and Learning:**

Biological growth and development are known as **Maturation.** Biological changes involve changes in the brain and the nervous system, which provide new abilities to a child. **Development proceeds from simple to complex.** In the beginning, a child learns through concrete objects and gradually moves to abstract thinking. This transition happens because of maturation.

Characteristics of Growth and Development:

Characteristics of Growth:

- It refers to an increase in size, length, height and weight.
- It is a function of an organism.
- It is intrinsic development.
- It follows direction and pattern.
- It does not continues throughout life. It stops after maturity.
- It refers to changes that can be quantified and measured in absolute terms.
- It is irreversible.
- It is a gradual process rather than saltatory.

• It is not uniform all through life.

• It may or may not bring development.

Characteristics of Development:

• It refers to overall changes in an organism.

• It continues throughout life.

• It implies improvement in functioning and behaviour.

• It brings qualitative changes, which are difficult to be measured directly.

• It is measured in relative terminal.

• It is reversible.

• It is determined by both heredity and environment.

• Development is also possible without growth.

Stages of Development:

It is useful to conceive of developmental periods, each Characterized by certain tasks to be accomplished. The failure to accomplish these developmental tasks is evidence of disease, either past or present.

Infancy:

At birth the infant is largely a reflex being equipped with primitive reflexes. Some of these, such as the rooting and sucking reflexes, are obviously utilitarian. It is generally true that most of the developmental milestones are first present in reflex from and then are modified as the developing central nervous system achieves peripheral connection through myelinization of the long spinal tracts. For example, the newborn infant has a firm reflex grasp. It requires about 4 months for the child to be able to reach out and seemed an object and then this is done only in a gross fashion, using chiefly the ulnar musculature. It will require another 2 months to be able to release an object held in the grasp; hence the ability to move an object from one hand to the other marks the middle of the first year. At about 9 to 10 months, thumb and finger apposition come into play, and the child becomes prehensile.

Development follows the principle of Cephalol –caudal differentiation as can easily be observed in the child's struggles to seize objects before the hand can be made to do the brains wishes. Social interplay, a cortical function, is well developed by 6 months when the child can just begin to move objects from hand to hand (shoulder girdle and cervical spine) and cannot yet usefully move the lower extremities (lumbar plexus and associated myotomes). Early speech sounds appear before ambulation is well established.

Evaluation of the very young sick infant is quite difficult because so few signs indicating disease are manifest. The social smile, the earliest sign of interpersonal interaction, appears only after about 4 weeks. Lack of even this rudimentary sign to aid an overall estimate of severity of illness commonly dictates that infants of lesser age be observed under hospital conditions until it becomes clear that no serious disease is present. Acquiring command of one's body is the major task of the first year.

Childhood:

Soon after the end of the first year, ambulation is well established. The newfound ability to leave mother ushers in the period known to most parents as the "terrible twos." The developmental task of this period is to discover and establish self- identity. For this reason, the child finds it difficult to accede to adult requests. It is essential to be established as an autonomous individual. Therefore the child cannot be agreeable, for if he or she always does the bidding of others, the fact of autonomous existence would not be firmly established. This is why it is usually futile for the examiner to try to coax a child of this age into cooperation. Firm, gentle mastery is more effective and more humane: the emerging personality is not required to lose face by yielding. Once the child has established independent existence, usually about the age of 3 years, he or she will become a friendly, amiable patient and will readily cooperate with all reasonable, nonthreatening requests.

Exploration of the environment and the interpersonal difficulties encountered with adults operate to make accident, trauma, and child abuse major health problems of this age group. Immunologic adaptations have also been changing. The young infant has certain passively acquired defenses against infectious disease that are lost toward the end of the first year. The effective replacement of this with artificial immunity and the supervision of the natural acquisition of disease resistance are major medical tasks. Until the newborn infant has lived with a recently acquired gut Flora for a while, the enteric organisms are an important hazard. The child's inability to respond to certain antigens results in vulnerability to encapsulated bacteria of the respiratory tract for the first few years, creating a spectrum of disease unique to this time of life.

Acquiring the skills for independent function within the family is the task of the next 3 years. Such things as toilet training, self- dressing, and eating behaviour are learned, and the difficulties encountered in this process are the common problems of life. Success in this phase is preparation for the next 10 years or so during which the task is to develop the capacity and skills necessary to function in our society. During these years society takes a leading role through its formalized training programs established for the young. Although the child is relatively free of acute disease, it is in these years that the slippage due to mental slowness, learning disability, chronic disease, and socioeconomic status begins to be manifest and to wreak it's secondary tolls.

Adolescence:

Adolescence, ushered in by the undeniable physiologic and anatomic changes of puberty, is Characterized by accelerating growth rates of the mesenchymal and reproductive tissues. These changes occur in females about 2 years earlier than in males. This growth spurt contains within itself, by endocrine feedback mechanisms, the seeds of its own termination. The wide range of normal developmental schedules requires great precision in descriptive terminology. To describe genitalia as "infantile" might be acceptable at an earlier age but will be entirely useless during this period when one normal 12 - year- old may be "infantile" and another " well developed." Tanner (1965) has described a staging of development that correlates the events of sexual development with the growth-rate curve and makes possible a quick and accurate recording of an individual's status. The use of Tanner staging is now the standard for this purpose.

The first task of adolescence is acceptance of a new body and the gender role that accompanies it. For many, this is a difficult task, one that must be approached gradually. Unisex clothing and other strategies useful in delaying the decisions required by development will be seen. Girls will be ladies one day and tomboys the next. The quiet boy who has difficulty taking on " macho" ways will be distressed. Normal differences in breast and genital size, even through temporary, cause problems.

The second task is separation from home and family and establishing oneself as an independent adult in society. This is just as important as separating from mother was at the age of 2 and can be equally unpleasant. It is difficult for parents to understand. It is difficult for parents to understand that by being parents they are disqualified as counselors for their own children, that there must be, at least symbolically, a revolution by which their child declares his or her independence, and that after this is accomplished, their relationship, however close,must be as adult to adult and not parent to child. The necessary separation does not come easy, and the child must seek a secure base outside the home; hence the importance of peer groups and the following of styles and fads and other means of allying with resources outside the home. The essence of these is that they must differ from those of the parent generation. Parents' efforts to join their adolescent children in these pursuits in ill- conceived attempts to be "buddies" are counterproductive. Unfortunately, this failure on the part of parents to understand normal development often leads the younger generation to adopt extreme tactics such as drug abuse, running away, or pregnancy to establish the point that must be made.

For females, the menarche is the best clinical sign that the patient has entered the last phase of declining rate of growth. Males will not enter this phase until 3 or 4 years later, and the event lacks such a clear clinical marker in their case. This cessation of growth marks a logical end of pediatrics, which by current convention is usually taken to be around age 18. For practical reasons, most pediatricians use high school graduation as a convenient marker, extending it in the case of patients suffering from marked developmental delay. This practice, of course, brings the pediatrician problem of gynecology, contraception, an occasional example of non- insulin- dependent diabetes mellitus (mature–onset diabetes of the young) and other problems more Characteristics of adult practice.

Conclusion:

Continual change is the essence of life. The cessation of growth at the end of adolescence is not the end of development. Development of physical prowess, skill, and the mental process continues for many years. Even middle-age does not interrupt development. Inevitably a process of involution begins. Like growth in earlier years, it affects different tissues and structures at different rates, slowed at first by the replacement of declining functions with newfound skills and bionic parts. Ultimately, however, change ceases – life ceases.

And so it is that no two patients with the same diagnosis have the same disease. Their problem formulations will be different, and their appropriate Management cannot be the same.

References:

- Knobloch H, Pasamanick B. Gesell and Amatruda's developmental diagnosis. New York: Harper & Row, 1974.
- Lowery GH. Growth and development of children. Chicago: Year Book Medical Publishers, 1978.
- Tanner JM. Growth at adolescence. 2nd end. Oxford: Blackwell, 1962.

- Tanner JM, Whitehouse RH, Takaishi M. Standards from birth to maturity for height, weight, height velocity, and weight velocity: British children, 1965. Arch Dis Children. 1966;41:613.
- Wetzel NC. In: Glasser O, Ed. Medical physics. Chicago: Year Book Medical Publishers, 1944.

CHAPTER V

EMOTIONAL PSYCHOLOGY: A STUDY OF DIFFERENT EMOTIONS

Tanwangini Sahani, Student, MBA (FA), GGSIPU, Delhi.

• • •

Introduction

Feelings and moods are frequently mistaken with emotions, but the three concepts are not identical. Emotion is defined as "a complex reaction pattern involving experiential, behavioural, and physiological elements," according to the American Psychological Association (APA). Emotions are how people react to issues or circumstances that are important to them. A subjective experience, a physiological response, and a behavioural or expressive response are the three key components of emotional states. Emotional experiences give rise to feelings. This is considered in the same category as hunger or pain because a person is aware of the sensation. An emotion produces a feeling, which can be impacted by memories, perceptions, and other variables. The American Psychological Association defines a mood as "any short-lived emotional state, usually of low intensity." Moods are distinct from emotions in that they lack stimulation and have no definite beginning point. Insults, for example, might elicit the emotion of rage, whereas an angry mood can emerge for no apparent reason.

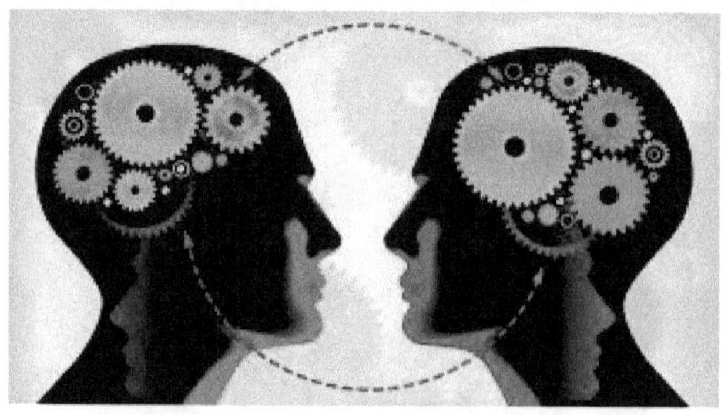

Figure 1: facebook.com

Emotion definition is still a work in progress. Many academics are still presenting theories regarding what makes up our emotions, and established theories are being challenged on a regular basis. Even so, there is a solid foundation of knowledge to examine when delving deeper into the subject. Emotion is commonly characterized in psychology as a complicated state of feeling that causes physical and psychological changes that affect thought and behaviour.

Emotionality is linked to a variety of psychological traits such as temperament, personality, mood, and motivation. Human emotion is defined as "physiological arousal, expressive behaviours, and conscious experience," according to author David G. Myers. We experience a wide range of emotions as we go about our daily lives. The term "emotion" refers to a subjective state of being that we commonly refer to as "feelings." Anger, contempt, fear, happiness, sadness, and surprise are the most fundamental emotions, sometimes known as the basic emotions. Basic emotions have a long evolutionary history in humans, and they evolved in part to aid us in making quick judgments about stimuli and guiding proper behaviour.

Objectives

- To know different types of emotions
- To study the components of emotions and the changes during emotions
- To understand how emotions influence Judgements.

Analysis and Discussion

Types of Emotions

There are several theories about how many different kinds of emotions people can have. Following are six universal emotions identified by psychologist Paul Eckman:

- Happiness is a pleasant emotion that causes people to feel a higher sense of well-being and contentment. Many people seek happiness. Smiling or speaking in an upbeat tone of voice are common ways to communicate happiness.
- Sadness is something that we all go through from time to time. Crying, being quiet, and/or withdrawing from others are all ways to communicate sadness. Grief, hopelessness, and disappointment are all examples of sadness.

- Fear can drive your heart to race, your mind to race, and your fight-or-flight reaction to kick in. It can be in response to real or perceived threats (something we think is threatening, but is actually not). Some people like the surge of adrenaline that comes with fear, whether it's from terrifying movies, roller coasters, or skydiving.

- Disgust is a bodily sensation that can be produced by rotten food, blood, or inadequate hygiene. When someone witnesses another person doing something they feel is immoral or disgusting, they may experience moral revulsion.

- Anger can be exhibited in a variety of ways, including frowning, yelling, or aggressive behaviour. Anger can push you to make positive changes in your life, but it's important to find a healthy outlet for it so that it doesn't harm you or others.

- Surprises can be both joyful and unpleasant. When you're astonished, you can open your lips or gasp. The fight-or-flight reaction can be triggered by surprise, just like it can be triggered by fear.

Figure 2:calmsage.com

1. **Components of Emotions**

- **Cognition:** This component mostly influences how we evaluate a situation, causing us to become emotionally involved in one manner or another, or even not.
- **Feeling:** We ponder about feelings in our daily lives. In an aroused person, the feelings are most immediately apparent alterations. Feelings have an instant motivating effect. They cause a variety of physiological changes in the cardiovascular system, including elevated blood pressure and alterations in sexual desire. They also elicit extensive electrochemical activity and excite the neurological system.
- **Behaviour:** Facial, postural, gestural, and vocal reactions are all part of the behavioural component.

Changes during Emotions

There are two types of changes that occur during emotions: external and internal changes.

- **External Changes**

During an emotional state, there are numerous outward or perceptible changes.

- The tone of the voice changes depending on the mood. Experiments have shown that emotions can be detected by listening to someone's voice.
- Changes in facial expressions occur. By looking at a person's face, we can tell what feeling he is experiencing.
- There will be changes in body language, such as muscle rigidity, finger-twisting, and hand and leg motions.
- Sweating.
- On the forehead, there are wrinkles.
- Eyes that are red.
- Hair erection on the skin, etc.

- **Internal Changes**

Many internal changes occur as a result of emotions. Stimulation is the cause of these internal changes. It is further subdivided into two parts. The sympathetic division prepares the body for emergency situations by fighting or fleeing, i.e. fighting if possible, fleeing if not. It stimulates the adrenal glands, causing an overabundance of adrenaline and noradrenaline to be released. Adrenaline circulates throughout the body, stimulating key organs and causing physiological changes.

- An increase in heart rate leads to a rise in blood pressure.
- Increased rate of respiration, increased blood sugar level, and decreased GI tract function—this is why we don't feel hungry when we're upset.
- Frequency changes in the brain
- pupillary dilation
- Saliva secretion is reduced, and the mouth is dry.

When the emergency or stressful crisis has passed, the next stage is to reclaim the energy that was expended throughout the emotional experience. The parasympathetic division is in charge of this task.

3. Emotions Influencing Judgements

Our emotional responses to our daily decisions may be helpful in focusing our attention on the most important things. However, intense emotions can cause us to make rash decisions.

Below are the nine ways in which your feelings might impact your decisions.

Figure 3: quora.com

- **A Narrow Mindset:** Strong emotions (such as wrath, anxiety, or hunger) cause "tunnel vision." Anger, for example, focuses attention in such a way that current sensations, thoughts, and impulses are given more weight than future objectives, desires, or plans.

- **Jumping to Conclusion:** An anxious person is motivated to eliminate uncertainty and discomfort. A selective information search, limited assessment of options, and speedy data evaluation guide the conclusion.
- **Attention Bias:** "What holds attention influences action," wrote William James. Individuals interpret information in ways that are congruent with their worldviews and self-perceptions. A person with low self-esteem, for example, is extremely sensitive to being neglected by others, and they are constantly on the lookout for signals that others do not like them.

- **Mood-Congruent Memory:** Our current emotional state aids in the memory of similar emotional experiences. We tend to recall positive occurrences when we are in a good mood and vice versa. This is due to the fact that different moods evoke distinct associations in the mind. Sad music is a powerful trigger for nostalgic thoughts of bygone eras for many people.
- **Emotional Contagion:** When we observe others' emotional expressions, we have a tendency to "catch" their emotions (sad or glad). This technique also aids us in comprehending others' feelings. When you have a casual discussion with someone who is worried, for example, you are likely to leave the meeting feeling uncomfortable as well.
- **Background Moods:** Emotions aroused by an incident that has nothing to do with a current scenario can have an impact on our thoughts and decisions. On brighter days, for example, we are more likely to tip at restaurants and exhibit higher levels of overall contentment.
- **An Urge to Blame:** We seek someone to blame for our misery when we are hurt and furious. We gain a sense of superiority by criticising others. It satisfies our ego to assume that any negative incident is the result of someone's fault.
- **Time Perception:** Emotions can cause time estimations to be skewed. We feel a slower passage of time while we are impatiently waiting for something to happen. When you're having a good time, time flies.
- **Projection Bias:** The majority of feelings are fleeting. What rises frequently falls. People, on the other hand, frequently underestimate the brief duration of emotional responses. People who are heartbroken, for example, are unable to predict how quickly their feelings would deteriorate. One of the reasons why adolescents are at such a high risk of suicide is that they lack the life experience to recognise that misery is just fleeting.

Recommendations and Findings

- Emotion emotions are a stage of neurobiological activity as well as the most important psychological/motivational part of emotion. They are the most important motivational mechanisms in humans.
- Emotional sentiments have a crucial role in the evolution, organisation, and operation of consciousness at various levels of awareness.

- Emotion management, influencing emotion-cognition relationships and developing high-level social skills all benefit from the capacity to symbolise and put feelings into words.
- Emotions are triggered quickly at first and can lead to quick action. However, once aroused, some emotions (for example, melancholy) might lead to more methodical thinking.
- Physiological response is triggered by an external stimulus. How you interpret those physical reactions determines your emotional response.
- At the same time, we sense emotions and physiological reactions including sweating, trembling, and muscle tightness.
- Changes in face muscles are strongly related to emotions. People who are forced to smile pleasantly at a social occasion, for example, will have a better time than those who frown or maintain a more neutral facial expression.

Conclusion

Every normal person has emotions. Perhaps we have felt all of the time, albeit at varying intensities. It is critical for us to notice, analyse, and respond to our own and others' feelings in order to understand ourselves and others. The centuries-old practice of seeking to make emotion and reason enemies, so marginalising sentiments, necessitates an abstraction that can only be successful if sensations are mild or ordinary in strength. Attempts to establish strong distinctions between body and awareness could be said to be analogous. The brain is an organ that communicates with the rest of the body.

Emotions can have a big impact on how you think and act. The emotions you experience on a daily basis can motivate you to act and influence the big and minor decisions you make in your life. Psychology is the scientific study of the mind and behaviour, and it encompasses a vast variety of human feelings, thoughts, and actions. Psychology has the ability to have a huge positive impact on people and societies.

References

- The Science Of Emotion: Exploring The Basics Of Emotional Psychology, https://online.uwa.edu/news/emotional
- The Experience of Emotion, https://opentextbc.ca/introductiontopsychology/chapter/10-1-the-experience-of-emotion/

- Emotions: (Definition and Components of Emotions), https://www.psychologydiscussion.net/notes/emotions-definition-and-components-of-emotions/666, Aman Sharma
- Emotions and Types of Emotional Responses, https://www.verywellmind.com/what-are-emotions-2795178, February 25, 2022, Kendra Cherry
- 9 Ways Your Emotions Influence Your Judgments, https://www.psychologytoday.com/us/blog/science-choice/201912/9-ways-your-emotions-influence-your-judgments, December 10, 2019, Ekua Hagan
- Emotion Theory and Research: Highlights, Unanswered Questions, and Emerging Issues, https://www.ncbi.nlm.nih.gov/pmc/articles/PMC2723854/,
- The 6 Major Theories of Emotion, https://www.verywellmind.com/theories-of-emotion-2795717, May 07, 2022, Kendra Cherry.

CHAPTER VI

PERSONALITY CONCEPTS AND THEORIES

Swati Singh, Student, B.Voc. Software Development,Guru Nanak Dev. Institute of Technology, Delhi.

• • •

INTRODUCTION

Personality Concept

Personality refers to a person's mental and physical well-being.

Davidson writes on temperament, that is socially developed once having a genetic base, through time in his medical textbook, "Principles and observe of drugs." once passing through a succession of biological process stages, the individual reaches associate adult psychological stage.

"Personality is that the most applicable conceptualization of a person's behaviour with all its characteristics, that the soul will offer in an exceedingly moment," McClelland says.

According to Davidson's conception, there area unit three completely different parts of one's temperament and its development and growth: social, physiological, and psychological.

McClelland has targeted on the psychological factors that influence desired changes in {an individual's|a person's|a temperament's|a human|somebody's} behaviour and personality.

As a result, each of those ideas shed some light-weight on the formation of temperament and individual behaviour. Excluding Allport's comprehensive approach to the topic, each of those definitions have the foremost application and utility in organisational behaviour.

An individual's temperament is exclusive, personal, and a primary issue of his behaviour.

Individuals answer completely different events in several ways that thanks to variances in temperament. Some temperament theorists highlight the necessity of recognising the person-situation interaction, i.e., personality's social learning parts. The study of human behaviour would profit greatly from such associate interpretation.

Source:Corporate Finance institute

Personality Nature

Every person's temperament is expounded to his or her nature. In general, someone asserts himself by his temperament traits. With their years of expertise, mature folks adopt associate objective perspective toward themselves et al.. They conjointly mirror on themselves so as to reinforce their temperament and behavior.

i. Self-Consciousness:

People at large and alternative species area unit immensely completely different. His temperament is marked by a attribute notable as'self-consciousness,' that permits him to remember of his surroundings and self-identity.

ii. Atmosphere Adaptability:

Off and on, temperament will build diversifications in response to desired changes. The term "resistance to change" refers to a disagreement defined by tension and conflict. folks sometimes comply with new surroundings and obstacles. Adaptation to new settings is usually in the middle of a modification in behaviour pattern, leading to a sleek operating condition and a nice atmosphere.

iii. Goal-oriented:

Folks try and accomplish their objectives. people do have the motivation to realize their objectives. Motive is that the results of needs and necessities. a person's want leads his or her behaviour toward achieving that want. activity changes area unit influenced by each physiological and social factors.

iv. Temperament Integration:

temperament works in an exceedingly consistent manner by combining varied activities (both mental and private experiences). temperament comes in an exceedingly kind of shapes and sizes. Temperament is differentiated by the style within which it's integrated. Folks with developed personalities have a powerful association to their values and experiences. This can be determined by their activity standards that they need developed from childhood.

Personality characteristics

You'll be asked to list your personal attributes if you apply for employment. Employers assume that your temperament is much fastened and will not vary considerably from year to year. Whereas most folks will relate to the current notion, wherever will our temperament originate? Is it in our polymer, or is it additional a results of our formative circumstances?

The answer is, of course, both. As a result of our brain and therefore the chemicals that act inside it area unit generated by genes, there area unit bound to be genes that influence our behaviour. Finding anybody of the many genes concerned, on the opposite hand, is notoriously tough. as a result of personalities area unit complicated, the biology of behaviour is as complicated.

Scientist's area unit solely currently commencing to gain a more robust understanding of however genes have an effect on behaviour.

i. Temperament is well-structured and consistent.

ii. Temperament may be a psychological attribute that's influenced by biological processes and necessities.

iii. Temperament influences however folks behave.

iv. Temperament is expressed in an exceedingly kind of ways that, together with thoughts, feelings, and behaviours.

Who Were the Neo-Freudians?

Many of the most tenets of Freud's psychotherapy theory were given by Neo-Freudian psychologists, however they updated and tailored the approach to accommodate their own beliefs, thoughts, and opinions. Scientist brain doctor instructed a spread of polemic views, however he conjointly no inheritable an oversized following.

Many of those students united with Freud's ideas regarding the unconscious and therefore the importance of childhood development. Alternative students, on the opposite hand, disagreed or outright rejected variety of things. As a result, these people developed their own distinct conceptions of temperament and psychological feature.

Neo-Freudian Disagreements

These neo-Freudian thinkers disagreed with neurologist for a spread of reasons. Erik Erikson, as an example, argued that brain doctor was mistaken in basic cognitive process that childhood events affected temperament virtually entirely. Alternative considerations that role player neo-Freudian philosophers' attention were:

The importance of sexual needs as a basic motive in Freud's theory

The absence of social and cultural influences on behaviour and temperament in Freud's work

Sigmund Freud's demoralised read on attribute

Many neo-Freudians believed that Freud's theories were too targeted on psychopathology, sex, and childhood events.

Instead, several of them selected to focus their theories on a lot of positive aspects of attribute moreover because the social influences that contribute to temperament and behavior.1

While the neo-Freudians might are influenced by Freud, they developed their own distinctive theories and views on human development, temperament, and behavior.

Major Neo-Freudian Thinkers

There were variety of neo-Freudian thinkers World Health Organization stone-broke with the brain doctor psychotherapy tradition to develop their own psychodynamic theories. a number of these people were at first a part of Freud's set, as well as Carl Jung and male monarch Adler.

Carl Jung

Carl Jung and Freud once had an in depth relationship, however Carl Gustav Jung stone-broke away to make his own concepts.2 Carl Gustav Jung observed his theory of temperament as analytical scientific discipline, and he introduced the conception of the collective unconscious. He delineated this as a universal structure shared by all members of an equivalent species containing all of the instincts and archetypes that influence human behavior.

Jung still placed nice stress on the unconscious, however his theory placed a better stress on his conception of the collective unconscious instead of the private unconscious. Like several of the opposite neo-Freudians, Carl Gustav Jung conjointly centered less on sex than Freud did in his work.

Alfred Adler

Alfred Adler believed that Freud's theories centered too heavily on sex because the primary incentive for human behavior.Instead, Adler placed a lesser stress on the role of the unconscious and a larger target social and social influences.

His approach, called individual scientific discipline, was focused on the drive that each one folks need to complete their feelings of inferiority. The complex, he urged, was somebody's feelings and doubts that they are doing not qualify to people or to society's expectations.4

Erik Erikson

While Freud believed that temperament was largely set in stone throughout time of life, Erikson felt that development continuing throughout life. He conjointly believed that not all conflicts were unconscious. He thought several were aware and resulted from the method|biological process} process itself.

Erikson de-emphasized the role of sex as a incentive for behavior and instead placed a far stronger target the role of social relationships.

His eight-stage theory of psychosocial development concentrates on a series of biological process conflicts that occur throughout the period of time, from birth till death. At every stage, folks face a crisis that has got to be resolved to develop sure psychological strengths.5

Karen Horney

Karen Horney was one amongst the primary girls trained in psychotherapy, and she or he was conjointly one amongst the primary to criticize Freud's depictions of ladies as inferior to men. Horney objected to Freud's portrayal of ladies as full of "penis envy."

Instead, she steered that men expertise "womb envy" as a result of they're unable involved youngsters. Her theory focuses on however behavior was influenced by variety of various neurotic desires.

Trait Theories of Personalities

Trait theorists believe temperament are often understood by positing that every one individuals have sure traits, or characteristic ways in which of behaving. does one tend to be sociable or shy? Passive or aggressive?

Optimistic or pessimistic? in keeping with the Diagnostic and applied mathematics Manual (DSM) of the yank medicine Association, temperament traits ar outstanding aspects of temperament that ar exhibited in an exceedingly wide selection of necessary social and private contexts. In alternative words, people have sure characteristics that partially confirm their behavior; these traits ar trends in behavior or angle that tend to be gift in spite of matters.

An example of a attribute is extraversion–introversion. sociableness tends to be manifested in outgoing, talkative, energetic behavior, whereas introversion is manifested in additional reserved and solitary behavior. a personal might fall on any purpose within the time, and therefore the location wherever the individual falls can confirm however he or she responds to varied things.

The idea of categorizing individuals by traits are often derived back as so much as Hippocrates; but additional fashionable theories have come back from Gordon Allport, Raymond Cattell, and Hans Eysenck.

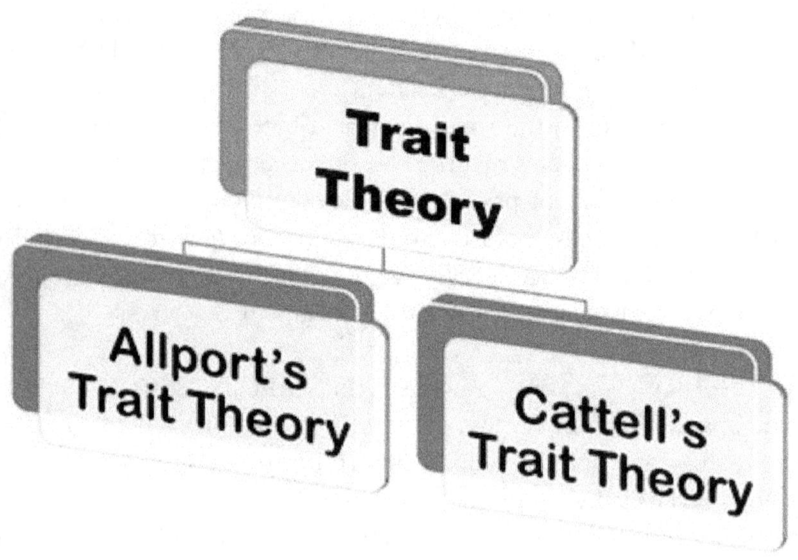

Source:Business Jargons

Gordon Allport (1897–1967)

Gordon Allport was one amongst the primary fashionable attribute theorists. Allport and Henry Odbert worked through 2 of the foremost comprehensive dictionaries of English language on the market and extracted around eighteen,000 personality-describing words. From this list they reduced the amount of words to roughly four,500 temperament-describing adjectives that they thought of to explain noticeable and comparatively permanent personality traits.

Allport organized these traits into a hierarchy of 3 levels:

Cardinal traits dominate Associate in Nursingd form an individual's behavior, like Ebenezer Scrooge's greed or Mother Theresa's unselfishness. They stand at the highest of the hierarchy and ar jointly referred to as the individual's master management. they're thought of to be Associate in Nursing individual's ruling passions. Cardinal traits ar powerful, however few individuals have personalities dominated by one attribute. Instead, our personalities ar generally composed of multiple traits.

Central traits come back next within the hierarchy. These ar general characteristics found in variable degrees in all and sundry (such as loyalty, kindness, agreeableness, friendliness, sneakiness, wildness, or grouchiness). They're the essential building blocks that form most of our behavior.

Secondary traits exist at all-time low of the hierarchy and don't seem to be quite as obvious or consistent as central traits. {they ar|they're} plentiful however are solely gift below specific circumstances; they embody things like preferences and attitudes. These secondary traits justify why someone might sometimes exhibit behaviors that appear incongruent with their usual behaviors. As an example, a friendly person gets Associate in Nursinggry once individuals attempt to tickle him; another isn't an anxious person however continuously nervous speaking in public feels.

Allport hypothesized that internal Associate in Nursing external forces influence an individual's behavior and temperament, and he stated these forces as genotypes and phenotypes. Genotypes ar internal forces that relate to however someone retains data and uses it to act with the globe. Phenotypes ar external forces that relate to the approach a personal accepts his or her surroundings and the way others influence his or her behavior.

Raymond Cattell (1905–1998)

In a trial to create Allport's list of four, 500 traits additional manageable, Raymond Cattell took the list and removed all the synonyms, reducing the amount right down to 171. However, speech communication that a attribute is either gift or absent doesn't accurately replicate a person's individuation, as a result of (according to attribute theorists) all of our personalities are literally created from constant attributes; we have a tendency to take issue solely within the degree to that every trait is expressed.

Cattell believed it necessary to sample a large vary of variables to capture a full understanding of temperament. The primary kind of knowledge was life knowledge that involves aggregation data from Associate in nursing individual's natural existence behaviors. Experimental knowledge involves activity reactions to standardized experimental things, and form knowledge involves gathering responses supported thoughtfulness by a personal concerning his or her own behavior and feelings. exploitation this knowledge, Cattell performed correlational analysis to generated sixteen dimensions of human temperament traits: preoccupancy, warmth, apprehension, emotional stability, liveliness, openness to alter, disposition, privateness, intelligence , rule consciousness , tension, sensitivity, social boldness, independence, vigilance, and dominance.

Based on these sixteen factors, he developed a questionnaire referred to as the 16PF. rather than a attribute being gift or absent, every dimension is scored over a time, from high to low. as an example, your level heatth|of heat} describes however warm, caring, and nice to others you're. If you score low on this index, you tend to be additional distant and cold. A high score on this index signifies you're corroboratory and comforting. Despite reducing considerably on Allport's list of traits, Cattell's 16PF theory has still been criticized for being too broad.

Hans Eysenck (1916–1997)

Hans Eysenck was a temperament theorizer World Health Organization targeted on temperament—innate, genetically primarily based temperament variations. He believed temperament is essentially ruled by biology, and he viewed individuals as having 2 specific temperament dimensions: sociableness vs. introversion and psychological disorder vs. stability. Once collaborating together with his married woman and fellow temperament theorizer Sybil H. J. Eysenck, he supplementary a 3rd dimension to the present model: psychoticism vs. socialization.

According to their theory, individuals high on the attribute of sociableness area unit sociable and outgoing and without delay connect with others, whereas individuals high on the attribute of introversion have the next have to be compelled to be alone, interact in solitary behaviors, and limit their interactions with others.

In the neuroticism/stability dimension, individuals high on psychological disorder tend to be associate degreexious; they have a tendency to possess an active sympathetic systema nervosum and even with low stress, their bodies and spirit tend to travel into a flight-or-fight reaction. In distinction, individuals high on stability tend to want additional stimulation to activate their flight-or-fight reaction and area unit so thought-about additional showing emotion stable.

CONCLUSION

The study of the theories of temperament is vital for college students because it prompts the requirement tounderstand why individuals behave as they are doing. Also, this space of study enlightens individuals on the requirement to be a lot of kind once judgement others supported however they behave since it's going to not be as a results of their own selection. The theories of privateity ar numerous relating to the character of personal behavior descriptions. additionally to the common theories, a reasonably uncommon conception, epigenetics is highlighted within the study of temperament theories. The range of personalities and therefore the relationships between the theories describing them points to the very fact that the human observation done by the theorists was correct to an oversized extent.

REFERENCES

- https://www.economicsdiscussion.net/management/personality/personality-introduction/32465
- https://www.verywellmind.com/who-were-the-neo-freudians-2795576
- https://courses.lumenlearning.com/boundless-psychology/chapter/trait-perspectives-on-personality/
- https://www.coursehero.com/file/p4t8mfk/Conclusion-The-study-of-the-theories-of-personality-is-important-for-students/#:~:text=described%20my%20personality.-,Conclusion%20The%20study%20of%20the%20t
- https://www.britannica.com/topic/personality
- https://www.verywellmind.com/what-is-personality-2795416
- https://courses.lumenlearning.com/boundless-psychology/chapter/introduction-to-personality/
- https://www.apa.org/topics/personality

CHAPTER VII

DUAL PERSONALITY OF Dr. JEKYLL

Dr. D. SASI DEVI,Assistant Professor in English, PG & Research Department of English,
Thiagarajar College , Affliated to Madurai Kamaraj University ,Madurai.

• • •

Introduction

Life on this earth is interesting because of its varied resources suitable to different tastes of every individual. Human beings enjoy the blessings of nature and also the goodness of every being. Yet, there is deterioration in the nature of man. Man does accept ethics, yet he finds it as a big challenge when he tries to face the world. He is affected mentally because of his baser instincts and his inability to lead a wishful life. At present we live in a world of utter chaos. Most of the individuals find themselves as an alien to their own selves; they lack an understanding of themselves and knowledge about the self is the core essence for happy survival. Unable to read their own mind at times they try to manipulate their own self and others. Under the canopy of society they act and reveal their good self. Darker wishes are nurtured in dark and it has a significant impact on the life. As time fleets one finds himself unable to manage with his negativity, and in turn loses his name and fame and eventually succumbs to evil and eventually meets with a pathetic end. All men do not have a harmonious balance of positive traits, they are a mixture of several traits and when there are abnormalities they are revealed as personality disorders.

Dual personality is a peculiar situation in which an individuals personality appears to have been separated into two or more distinct personalities each with its own complex characters and distinct organisation. Each would have its own self identity and perceptions. Scientists and philosophers have largely quoted that the role of heredity and environment play a vital role in shaping human behaviour. This word 'Dualism' has its root in the Latin word *duo* which refers to two. The existence of two diverse characters in a single person is termed as split personality or dual personality. R.L.Stenevenson was a Scottish novelist, a short story writer and poet much interested in the working of the mind. He proves to be an excellent craftsman of the novella " *The strange case of Dr.Jekyll and Mr Hyde.*" The author adopts a wonderful narration to portray the dual nature of the main character Dr. Jekyll. The first eight chapters are in third person narrative and the last two chapters are in the form of letters. He employs the final chapter to unravel the mysterious mystery and also to impart the moral which he already had in store while fabricating the novella. It is a much explored novella and it holds relevance to the modern era.

As a lawyer R.L.Stevenson showed immense interest in criminal practice. He read a lot about trials in Scotland. Along with Edmund Gosse, he wrote a series of papers on murder trials. It was not a surprise when his interest found its way in his creative writing "The Suicide Club" (1882), "Markheim" (1885) and "Olalla" (1885). R.L. Stevenson has closely examined the workings of deviant mind. Just then, in the Victorian Age, tales regarding abnormal behaviour was getting popularised. Stevenson's close friendship with the psychologist James Sully and his knowledge about his essay *"Genius and Insanity"* enriched his knowledge. He happily owned a copy of Charles Darwin's "The Expression of the Emotions in Man and Animals" (1872). Author showed his keen interest in disordered mental states. He also wrote a review to Edgar Allan Poe's collected tales; he praised the author profusely for his unbelievable insights into the most debatable concept of sanity and insanity. His wide knowledge about behavioural pattern through various sources helped him to beautifully fabricate his novella.

In *"The strange case of Dr. Jekyll and Mr Hyde"* Dr. Jekyll is a modest, well respected, successful, brilliant and intellectual man. He is a prominent character of this novella with a sinister figure of unknown origin. Mr. Gabriel Utterson and Mr. Enfield are the characters who struggle to study the plight of Dr. Jekyll and his relationship with the ominous Hyde. Lanyon plays a small role yet a very vital role. Butler Poole has a significant course of action.

Mr.Utterson and Mr.Enfield are reserved and enjoy walking together without a word in silence. They are much disturbed to see Hyde trample on the young girl. They share mutual dislike for gossip, hence they do not involve in the discussion about the identity of Hyde once they understand that he is an individual familiar to Mr.Utterson. In general Mr.Utterson is intrigued by the darker side of the world. He is an embodiment of rationality and dismisses fancy and becomes a representative of common sense approach. In true words, Hyde's ugliness is not only physical but it relates to the metaphysical existence. It has more to do with his soul rather than the physical appearance and the nature of the body. Enfield and Utterson's nature is not of the meta physical plane and hence they sense Hyde's deformity and uncanniness yet both are unable to describe the ugliness. The eerie and the inexplicable have no expression in words. Language fails to explain since imagination has lesser role in the mind of Enfield and Utterson.

As a friend and lawyer Utterson possesses the will of Dr.Jekyll. He checks the will. It states "all his possessions were to pass into the hands of his "friend and benefactor Edward Hyde"; but in case of Jekyll's disappearance or unexplained absence for any period exceeding three calendar months, the said Edward Hyde should step into the said Henry Jekyll's shoes without further delay, and free from any burthen or obligation, beyond payment of a few small sums to the members of the doctor's household." (Stevenson 20) This strange will had disturbed Utterson for a long time and now after coming to know something about Hyde's behaviour, he is totally shattered and is now intrigued by the peculiar strange power of Hyde over his friend Dr.Jekyll. Lanyon and Jekyll had moved away on a professional dispute.

Utterson encounters Hyde and greets him and introduces him as a good friend of Dr. Jekyll and in his anxiety to know more he visits his friend Jekyll on the same day. Jekyll is not to be found. But he learns from the butler Mr. Poole that Hyde has a key to the laboratory and all the servants were ordered to obey Hyde. Immediately Utterson assumes that Hyde is main culprit who is blackmailing Jekyll for some wrong done during his adolescence or childhood days.

After a fortnight Utterson attends Dr.Jekyll's dinner and stays long after the party wishing to have a very personal conversation. During the meet he makes a passing reference to the key details mentioned in the will and gently reveals his knowing about the character Hyde. "The large handsome face of Dr. Jekyll grew pale to the very lips, and there came a blackness about his eyes. " I do not care to hear more," said he. "This is a matter I thought we had agreed to drop" (32) Jekyll also continued to say that "I am painfully situated, Utterson; my position is a very strange one. It is one of those affairs that cannot be mended by talking." (32) Utterson takes up the role of a amateur detective. His doubts are further strengthened by the wills reference to disappearance. He further develops that Jekyll might be murdered or kidnapped and hence the use of such strange word disappearance.

Utterson has a sequence of dreams. Actually it is a technique employed by R.L. Stevenson to enlighten Utterson. In his dreams faceless figure dominates. He identifies it as Hyde. The figure just walks through the London city. Every time he dozed over, he only did to see Hyde moving swiftly or gliding stealthily. Hyde appears to be ubiquitous character, permeating and filling the whole city with his dark nature. He is a symbolic representation of all the secret sins one nurtures. At one point Utterson calls this figure as 'troglodyte' a prehistoric man who lived in the caves.

Sir Danvers Carew, a popular member of the parliament is murdered and a letter is found in his pocket addressed to Utterson. The lady who witnessed the murder indentifies the murderer as Hyde. He proceeds with police to meet Hyde. He lives in such a pathetic squalor and shockingly he is the heir of Henry Jekyll's fortune. Weapon used for murder is found there but not the murderer. Police trace that he has accounts in bank. They wait for his visit in vain. None knows about him except his evil and ugly disposition.

Jekyll makes up his mind and makes a firm decision in mind, then claims that Hyde has left his life forever and their relationship has ended. A letter handed by Jekyll to Utterson throws a little light over the commotion. Utterson consults with an expert in handwriting to find the owner of that writing. It is revealed that it is the handwriting of Jekyll which Jekyll had forged for the sinister murderer Hyde. Hyde is not only an opportunist manipulating Jekyll but he was capable of violent murder with no motive. Time fleets, no sign of Hyde to be seen. Jekyll seems to regain his health. He becomes sociable and gives himself much to charity. Utterson sees that the disappearance of Hyde promotes Jekyll's health and there is a lot of remarkable improvement.

Jekyll throws a dinner party and all his friends come together and celebrate happiness and togetherness. Later Utterson calls Jekyll and learns that he does not entertain any visitor or a friend. After several failed attempts to meet Jekyll, he meets Dr. Lanyon . He is on his death bed looking pale and weak. His sickly pale looks make one frightened. Lanyon discloses that he had a great shock and is unable to accept it. He foresees his death very shortly. On the other hand he did not wish to explain things. He refused to speak or discuss anything about Jekyll and subtly expressed his deep hatred for his one time friend Dr. Jekyll. After Lanyon's death as prophesied Utterson receives a letter meant to be opened after Lanyon's death. It again had an instruction to wait until the death of Dr. Jekyll.

During their usual walk Utterson and Enfield peer into Jekyll's home. Surprisingly Jekyll is found at his window watching eagerly. He takes delight in conversing with his friends and complains that he feels low. Yet, he was not ready to come out of his residence for a feel of fresh air. He refused to set right his physical discomfort. He wanted free air but was not ready to come out and be with nature. Just then , on Jekyll's face a strange terror swept in, he hurriedly shut his windows and vanished even without bidding a goodbye. The two friends were shocked but in silence they departed.

Butler Poole visits Utterson and expresses his doubt of a foul play regarding his master Dr. Jekyll and Hyde. He seeks the help of Utterson and brings him home. Utterson asks for permission to meet his friend Jekyll. Jekyll refuses but the refusal was not in his voice, it was strangely awful. Utterson was confused and he became totally anxious about the safety of his friend. He assumes that someone or probably Hyde had murdered Jekyll. He wonders why the murderer has not escaped from the spot. This greatly disturbs and confuses him. Poole discloses that this strange voice has commanded him and sent him to the chemist and druggist store for the purchase of some chemical ingredient. Utterson comes to a consensus that Jekyll might have contracted some uncommon disease which would have transformed his voice and deformed his physical appearance to an unrecognisable extent. He is totally denied by Poole for he assures that the person was very small compared to Dr. Jekyll his master and he also added that he was similar to Hyde.

Butler Poole and Utterson resolve to break in. Initially they demand for admittance. The strange voice begs for mercy and it resembles Hyde. After some discussion on these confusions they break open only to find Hyde lying on the floor. He too seems sickly. The whole building is ransacked for Jekyll. But, the search goes in vain. A large mirror was found in the lab, and it was a strange item for a laboratory. A large envelope was placed on the table and it had important messages. The first one was Jekyll's will. But, matter had undergone a change, Hyde's name was replaced by Utterson. This is a unbelievable positive change. The second is a note to Utterson. He remains bewildered. His mind is filled with the question whether Dr. Jekyll has murdered Hyde. He stays peace less. Utterson was instructed to read the letter delivered by Lanyon. Utterson finds himself utterly helpless. He tries to resolve the matter of Jekyll and Hyde. But, it seems like a complicated maze. Utterson could not be blamed for the situation was more challenging.

The last and the final chapter revels that Jekyll was a hard working, healthy man who possessed a large inheritance and remained a decent man. He was an ideal man and maintained a respectable disposition. He was forced to hide his frivolous and indecent side. As a mature person he realised that he was leading a dual life. His learned nature and his deep interest lead him to dive deep into mystical studies. He explored about the divided nature or the dual personality of a man. He believed that a man is truly two and not one on the basis of the existing goodness and evil nature. As a well learned and a knowledgable Scientist Jekyll involved himself in much research. After several experiments he secretly enjoyed his success in discovering a peculiar potion to serve his secret dark purpose. Later there was no time left to reverse, he realised that he has risked his life and it was too late. However, he tried he could not retrieve his path and claim his own self, as his original self.

The entire process of experiment and even the success is not a pleasant experience, his passion was burning and hence he sacrificed and toiled hard. He underwent immeasurable pain, nausea and an untold mysterious misery. Physically he found himself shrunken and deformed totally into a different personality revealing his inner dark side He had a very shabby obnoxious ugly disposition. He assumed that his shorter stature as Hyde and considered it as his repressed dark nature. Unknowingly, without knowing much of his ill fate he welcomed his crude transformation behind the screens. He enjoyed and loved to remain as Hyde. Jekyll entertained him well; furnished him a home fulfilling his taste. Opened a bank account and made all comforts for befitting his interests.

In the name of Hyde he was free to do his will and express his baser feelings. He was never accountable for his unscrupulous deeds. He would immediately get transformed to Jekyll and this individual never had an iota of ill feeling, a sense of shame, guilt for all the undue exploits he would have incurred in the name of Hyde. He never felt sorry and never tried to amend things. Life was smooth and this happy life continued for a considerable length of time. This became questionable only when his physique started to change even without his permission and knowledge. The transformation which was aided by the potion was of no use, without the help of the potion he changed and it baffled him. One day he was shocked to see himself as Hyde when he got up from bed in the morning. This was a warning bell and he realised it as a deadly signal. He decided to stop the game for he might he trapped by the police as Hyde for all his past atrocities. Lesson remained good for two months, then he took the potion again. It unleashed the darker energy with full force. It emerged as a wild savage full of vengeance. This is when Carew is beaten to death to the highest delight of Hyde. Hyde has no iota of remorse. Again Jekyll took a second lesson not to transform anymore and it was when he had party with Utterson and Enfield.

As days passed Jekyll grew tired and weary of his constant virtuous life. He found it tasteless and hence tried to indulge again in certain dark desires in shade. His involvement in the dark desires was more than sufficient to provoke his transformation without any drug. Jekyll was at leisure in a park and he got transformed unknowingly. What was amazingly welcome was, as Hyde he felt enormously powerful and bold. Yet, he was aware that he would be seized for murdering Carew. With the help of Lanyon, he took double dose every six hours to avoid the spontaneous transformation into Hyde. It was during such spells he withdrew himself and shut the window when he was talking to Utterson and Enfield through the window.

Astonishingly one finds Jekyll growing weaker and Hyde growing stronger towards the end. The chemical in the drug store was running out of stock and the new stock purchased did not have the same earlier effect. Jekyll was puzzled and hence assumed that the earlier drug could have had some impurities which made it work. To his dismay he felt that he might permanently become Hyde with no chance of transforming.

All the mysteries start unravelling. So far the reader had Utterson's point of view and now there is a change in the view. Readers face what was happening through Dr. Jekyll's point of view and sometimes through Hyde. The shift in the point of view makes the difference. All the mysterious, shrouded, puzzling events are clearly revealed one after the other.

As the novella proceeds one notices that there is reversal of what was expected. His darker side gains energy and grow stronger and stronger until the original mixture of good and evil of Jekyll stops to exist. On the physical plane Hyde is smaller in stature. This Jekyll mistakes for being younger and he assumes that evil is small in him and under developed than his good self. On the other hand the physical strength of Hyde was superior. It was vigorously powerful. Hyde does acts of crime and Jekyll never feels for it though Hyde is his own creation

Dr.Jekyll is a mixture of good and evil. The willingness on the part of Jekyll to get convinced that he does not have the responsibility for the acts of Hyde shows the cruelty of Dr.Jekyll. With this the reader comes to know that Jekyll represents each and every human being and each one tries to keep his or her own evil (Hyde) under control. They love evil and they are secretly fascinated by such acts yet they are restricted by their moral constraints and social norms.

In the novella R. L. Stevenson has the liberty to express his own analysis of insanity and its implications. Dr.Jekyll the creation of R.L.Stevenson is a peculiar man who succumbs to bouts of madness. His cognitive faculties are not affected. Jekyll suffers from disordered emotional and volitional faculties and hence gets transformed to Hyde. This Victorian novel was written much ahead of its time. It throws a clear light on the concept of goodness and evil nature which exist in every human being. It is in other words, a study about the hypocrisy and the double standards of the present society. It is also an in depth study and analysis of human psyche.

BIBLIOGRAPHY

* Stevenson, R L. *The Strange case of Dr. Jekyll and Mr. Hyde.* New York: Bantam Books.1981.
* Guttenplan S, editor. *A companion to the philosophy of mind.* Oxford: Blackwell.1996.

CHAPTER VIII

BEHAVIOURAL FINANCE: STUDY OF THE IMPACTS OF PSYCHOLOGY ON INVESTORS AND FINANCIAL MARKETS

Hardik Sawhney, Risk Analyst, Credit Suisse, Mumbai.

• • •

Introduction

The first Indian mega start-up Zomato, despite being a loss-making company for three consecutive financial years received a hearty reception from the Indian investors. On the 23rd of July, the shares of the food start-up made a stellar debut by opening at a premium of nearly 53%. Regardless of the statements by company officials about increasing future expenses and falling revenues in the upcoming time, the overjoyed welcome was an example of the herd mentality. But what now? Several warnings by some market enthusiasts of the IPO being overpriced is now kicking some action. The stock which hit the high at 168 mark is now struggling to equate to its issue price of 76.

Figure1: thestreet.com

The timing of the food unicorn's entry into the market can be referred to as a perfect example of the exploitation of psychological effects on investors and financial markets.

Market psychology can be defined as a macroeconomic behaviour in which emotions and sentiments overpower rational thinking. The theory of efficient market hypothesis (EMH) by two of the greatest American economists Fama and Samuelson have been widely criticised due to the non-inclusion of the adequate psychological factor. The theory states that all participants in the market behave rationally and not emotionally. But what ideally happened? The ideal-looking, fair-priced food delivery stock saw a free fall, the United States housing bubble also called the greatest financial crisis took place shaking the world economy and many more.

This irrational behaviour was hard to explain and many financial economists had been struggling to identify the extent of such faulty judgements by the investors. The term Behavioural finance can be used to explain this deviation from standard behaviour. Economist Amos Tversky and Nobel prize-winning Psychologist Daniel Kahneman populated the theory of behavioural finance which aimed in identifying the errors in investors' decision-making due to cognitive biases such as overconfidence, herd mentality and loss aversion.

The theory gained huge popularity and elevated levels of recognition due to its realistic functioning. And even today many traders, hedge fund managers and financial institutions enjoy the advantages of market mispricing due to investor psychology and behavioural finance.

Objectives

- To understand the theory of behavioural finance and theories related to the investor at Macro and Micro levels.
- To know how theories can be used as a tool, by the players and financial institutions to gain benefits.

Analysis and Discussion

Behavioural Finance

For several years, the financial and economic literature relied upon the theory of the efficient market hypothesis which states that the market participants behave rationally and irrationally, where irrational behaviour is balanced by the irrational behaviour of some other market participant. Therefore, leaving no space for sentiments and cognitive errors. This meant that the markets are efficient in themselves and however extreme the situations may be, the significant decisions of the market will stay unaffected. The EMH model has been widely accepted and appreciated by several economists and financials However there have been instances where the non-standard behaviour has been quite visible.

To understand this irrationality, studies from the field of Cognitive psychology were inculcated into the financial world. Ultimately, it was found that fusing psychological factors in the macroeconomic models confirms the prediction of non-standard behaviour of market participants.

Figure 2: leverageedu.com

Behavioural finance is the mix of sociological and psychological factors which can deviate from rational behaviour and affect the market as a whole. This theory is extremely popular and celebrated in the global markets today due to real-life evidences.

According to EMH, investors are risk-averse and hold optimal and well-diversified portfolios. However, behavioural finance tells how investors in the real world make financial decisions, and how they are affected by cognitive and sentimental faults.

- **Prediction And Exploitation Of Market Psychology**

There are two conventional methods which are employed by the majority of investors for employing stock picking.

1. The fundamental analysis investigates the stocks by using sources such as financial statements and industry-oriented reports.
2. The technical analysis seeks out-trend levels, indicators, and various candlestick charting techniques. Here market psychology is one of the factors which can affect the pricing in the market.

Large institutions engaged in the hedge fund, primarily use the psychological factor as they are engaged in exploiting the gap between fundamentals and market mentality for profit-making.

Even at micro levels with the help of doing extensive research and appropriate knowledge one can predict the market's true behaviour and oppose herd psychology. Investors who engage in such situations are referred to as Contrarian investors. Warren Buffet, one of the most successful investors of all time is one of them.

Theories as a Tool to Gain Benefits

Further, to obtain a better understanding of the theories, take a look at the case study below, which will assist in analysing how the theories can be applied to benefit various stakeholders in the financial markets, including financial institutions, in the current environment.

Case Study

The finance ministry in its annual budget statement held on the very first day of February every year kept Life Insurance Corporation of India's (LIC) IPO as one of the major highlights. In the 2022 discussion, our finance minister Ms Nirmala Sitharaman gave a green light to launch the insurance giant IPO. Every listener ranging from a market investor to various lively roles was fascinated by this crowd puller.

Receiving such a positive assurance from the Govt. of India, even the proportion of the national population which were never into the financial markets, thought of becoming potential investors as to be insured by the central authority itself instead of the insurance company LIC. Many sources cited that the number of Demat account openings saw a sudden upsurge in response to the eagerness for the IPO.

However, the stock was heard singing a different tune in its pre-listing days. The IPO which had all eyes while entering the market has not been the brightest star which everyone was hoping it to be. The stock, despite being marked as one of the most fairly priced by a majority of the market enthusiasts, listed at a discount of approximately 8.6% from its allotment price of Rs. 949. The stock continues to slump and on the day of writing (10 June 2022), the stock touched an all-time low of Rs.708.

So, what went wrong? Was there some planning behind its launch? Do the government and central bank have any motive?

These questions cannot be answered without any statistical data however there are a certain points that can be noticed and observed.

After the Covid outbreak of 2019, the inflationary situation of our economy has not been in a good shape. The monetary policy of the committee of the Reserve Bank of India mentioned the consumer price inflation level index touching its peak in January 2022, in one of their reports.

With already having targets of disinvestment, there could have been no way better to use LIC IPO for killing two birds with a stone. So, using the advantage of the herd mentality bias an idea could be formed that the Government and the Central bank of India tightened up the money supply of the economy by making people inadvertently invest, which in turn may have resulted in lowering the levels of inflation. This can be thought of as a perception however the outcome of the same would have been in the Central authority's favour.

Recommendations and Findings

- Behavioral finance is a branch of finance that studies how psychological factors influence market outcomes and can be used to assess various outcomes in a range of sectors and enterprises.
- Loss aversion occurs when investors place a higher value on the fear of losing money than the joy of making money. In other words, they're considerably more inclined to prioritise minimising losses over maximising investment returns.
- All sorts of market anomalies, particularly market anomalies in the stock market, such as significant spikes or declines in stock price, can be explained by influences and biases.
- As evident from some of the recent incidents, the findings show that behavioural finance and market psychology has a significant impact on an investor's decision-making process. In addition to this, the animal behaviour of herd mentality has been one of the most prominent reasons for the irrational behaviour of market participants.
- Following the cases of Zomato, and LIC IPO, it can be understood that many market participants with their assessment and own research gain advantages of market inefficiencies because of psychological factors of the mass and inculcate the same in their financial models.
- The investor's mental and physical health often plays a role in financial decision-making. As an investor's general health improves or deteriorates, so does their mental state. This has an impact on their decision-making and reasoning in all real-world situations, including

financial ones.

Conclusion

Behavioral finance can be examined from a number of angles. Stock market returns are one area of finance where psychological factors are frequently considered. So, just as the market isn't always efficient, humans aren't always rational. Behavioral finance can assist in understanding why people don't always make the right decisions, and why markets might be unreliable at times. It is somewhat referred to as a relatively new field as compared to the traditional approaches. However, the practicality of the theory has gained huge acceptance in the financial world. Having the advantage of being a modern theory some limitless approaches and findings are, yet to be discovered in the field. The human sentiment at micro and macro economical levels can vary following a new situation every time. Such complexity of human behaviour is tough to interpret in exact terms. Nonetheless, incorporation of some broader factors such as Anchoring, Overconfidence and loss aversion biases have been doing the trick.

Figure 3: proschoolonline.com

One thing that needs to be noted is that the failure of the Efficient Market Hypothesis highlights a major flaw in the financial world. This inefficiency is answered by behavioural finance and market psychology. Individuals can make smart decisions and earn higher returns if they understand the biases that influence their decision-making. It can also assist in forming successful wealth management plans.

References

- Inflation may have peaked in January: RBI deputy governor Michael Patra, https://www.business-standard.com/article/economy-policy/inflation-may-have-peaked-in-january-rbi-deputy-governor-michael-patra-122022400071_1.html, February 24, 2022, Manojit Saha
- Behavioral Finance, https://www.investopedia.com/terms/b/behavioralfinance.asp, May 24, 2022, Adam Hayes
- Behavioural finance –(definition, importance & themes), https://www.proschoolonline.com/blog/behavioural-finance-a-subject-to-be-cherished
- What is Behavioral Finance and how does it affect your Financial decisions?, https://blog.finology.in/behavioral-finance/what-is-behavioral-finance, 14 Sep 2020

CONCEPT OF PERSONALITY,TYPES, TRAITS AND ADJUSTMENT

Pranati das,Student, Meerabai Institute of Technology,Maharani Bagh,GGSIPU,Delhi.
Dr.Archana Deshpande,Associate Professor,Guru Nanak Institute of Management,GGSIPU, Delhi.

• • •

Introduction

At its most fundamental level, personality refers to a person's distinctive patterns of thoughts, feelings, and behaviors. Personality is said to emerge from within an individual and to be consistent throughout life.

We can see examples of personality in how we characterize other people's characteristics. "She is giving, loving, and a little bit of a perfectionist," for example, or "They are devoted and protective of their friends."

The term "personality" is derived from the Latin word "persona," which refers to a theatrical mask worn by actors to project multiple parts or conceal their identity. From a broad perspective, personality refers to an individual's entire personality. It encompasses a person's physical, mental, and emotional well-being.

Personality is the impression of distinguishing characteristics that makes an individual stand out. It is the sum of an individual's physical, psychological, and behavioral characteristics that contribute to his 'good personality or lack thereof, depending on the presence or absence of characteristic features.

Personality – Concept:

Personality refers to an individual's mental and physical well-being. Davidson writes on personality, which is socially developed after having a genetic base, through time in his medical textbook, "Principles and Practice of Medicine." After passing through a succession of maturational stages, the individual reaches an adult psychological stage.

An individual's personality is unique, personal, and a primary factor of his behavior. Individuals respond to different situations in different ways due to variances in personality. Some personality theorists highlight the need of recognizing the person-situation interaction, i.e., personality's social learning components. The study of human behavior would benefit greatly from such an interpretation.

According to Davidson's concept, there are three different components of one's personality and its development and growth: social, physiological, and psychological. McClelland has focused on the psychological factors that influence desired changes in an individual's behavior and personality.

As a result, both concepts shed some light on the formation of personality and individual behavior. Apart from Allport's comprehensive approach to the subject, both definitions have the most applicability and utility in organizational behavior. An individual's personality is unique, personal, and a primary factor of his behavior.

Individuals respond to different situations in different ways due to variances in personality. Some personality theorists highlight the need of recognizing the person-situation interaction, i.e., personality's social learning components. The study of human behavior would benefit greatly from such an interpretation.

Personality – Nature:

Every person's personality is related to his or her nature. In general, a person asserts himself by his personality traits. With their years of experience, mature people adopt an objective perspective toward themselves and others. They also reflect on themselves in order to enhance their personality and behavior.

- **Self – Conscious: -**

There is a significant distinction between humans and other species. His nature is marked by 'self-consciousness,' which allows him to be aware of his surroundings and self-identity.

- **Adaptability to the environment: -**

Off and on, personality does make adaptations in response to desired changes. Change resistance entails a conflict that is tense and unpleasant. People usually adjust to new surroundings and obstacles. Adaptation to new settings is frequently accompanied by a change in behavior patterns, resulting in a smooth working condition and a pleasant environment.

- **Goal-oriented:**

People struggle to attain their objectives. Individuals do have the motivation to pursue their objectives. Motive is the result of desires and wants. An individual's desire leads his or her behaviour toward achieving that desire. Behavioral changes are influenced by both physiological and social factors.

- **Integration of Personality;**

Personality is consistent because it integrates many activities (both mental and personal experiences) into one. Personality is differentiated by the way it is integrated. People with developed personalities have a strong connection to their values and experiences. This is determined by their behavioural standards, which they have developed from childhood.

How Personality Develops

There are numerous theories regarding personality, and many of these views are influenced by different schools of psychology. Some theories focus on how personalities are expressed, while others are more concerned with how they evolve.

Personality Type:

According to type theories, there are only a few personality types that are linked to biological factors.

According to one view, there are four different sorts of personalities. They are as follows:

Type A: - Impatient, competitive, work-obsessed, achievement-oriented, aggressive, and stressed Perfectionist, impatient, competitive, work-obsessed, achievement-oriented, aggressive, and stressed.

Type B: - Low stress, even temperament, flexibility, creativity, adaptability to change, patience, procrastination tendencies.

Type C: - Highly conscientious, a perfectionist who finds it difficult to express emotions (positive and negative).

Type D: - Worrying, depressed, impatient, pessimistic, negative self-talk, social avoidance, lack of self-confidence, fear of rejection, appears dismal, hopeless.

The Myers-Briggs personality type hypothesis is another popular personality type theory. The Myers-Briggs Personality Type Indicator determines a person's personality by measuring where they fall on four different continuums: introversion-extraversion, sensing-intuition, thinking-feeling, and judging-perceiving.

Personality Traits:

Personality, according to trait theories, is the outcome of internal genetically based qualities such as:

- **Agreeable:** - Someone who is concerned about others, has empathy, and enjoys assisting others.
- **Conscientiousness:** - Goal-directed activities, high levels of thinking, and effective impulse control
- **Eager to Please:** - Accepting, passive, and conforming are three words that come to mind while thinking of accommodating, docile, and conforming.
- **Extraversion:** - Excitement, sociability, talkativeness, assertiveness, and a high level of emotional expressiveness are all desirable traits.
- **Introversion:** - restrained and quiet
- **Neuroticism:** - Has a lot of stress and mood swings, is worried, worries about a lot of things, gets angry easily, and has a hard time recovering from stressful events.

Psychoanalytical theory of Personality: -

The psychoanalytic ideas of personality will be discussed in this article.

- **Sigmund's Theory of Personality: -**

Psychoanalysis was founded by Sigmund Freud (1856-1939). His psychoanalysis theory is dynamic, and it is founded on the concept that personality and personality development are shaped by conflicts and events that are mostly unconscious in nature and can only be comprehended via in-depth investigation.

The id, ego, and super ego are all concepts in Sigmund Freud's anatomy of personality. Each of these personality traits is linked to the other two. Personality is divided into three categories: Id, Ego, and Super ego. The Id is completely unconscious, the Ego is partially awake, and the Super Ego is completely aware.

The Id is the most important part of a person's personality. Id, according to Freud, is a jumble of unconscious tendencies. It is not organized in a logical manner. Indeed, it is possible for opposing urges to coexist in it. Id has no morals. It has no concept of what is valuable. It can't tell the difference between good and evil. The pleasure principle is in charge. The processes of the Id are unconscious. The unconscious, conative part of personality is best described as id.

Because so much of a person's personality operates at the unconscious level, Freud assumed that the only way to bring it to the surface of consciousness is to use the approach of Free Association. He also saw dream analysis as a valuable tool for delving into the unconscious mind's contents.

They help to relieve the stress that comes with not being able to satisfy one's demands. It is general knowledge that a newborn baby expects to be gratified or to have his wants met (hunger, warmth and elimination, etc.).

Libido and Infantile Sexuality:

Libido is the component of the Id system that derives pleasure solely from sexual engagement. Sexual enjoyment, like other gratifications, should be regarded as a normal human need. It was defined by Sigmund Freud as an organism's whole striving. Even in infants, desire was present in the organism, according to Freud. Every child is born with a level of sexual excitability that is physiologically defined.

Libido can be stimulated through the following zones: -

• **Oral Zone: -**

From birth to the age of two years. Sucking the lips gives the baby pleasure at this age.

• **Anal Zone: -**

Between the ages of two and three. Anal expulsion or manipulation gives the child a lot of pleasure.

• **Genital Zone: -**

The child gets pleasure from caressing his genitals when he is 3 to 5 years old.

- **Latency Zone: -**

The latency stage lasts from the age of six to around thirteen, and it is characterized by the avoidance of sexuality due to societal constraints.

- **Fixation Stage: -**

The latency stage lasts from the age of six to around thirteen, and it is characterized by the avoidance of sexuality due to societal constraints.

Most Freud's patients suffered from sex repression, or the lack of sex enjoyment. The ability to sublimate sexual desires aids in the development of a well-rounded personality.

- **Evaluation of Freud's theory:**

The personality theory of Sigmund Freud is extremely useful in understanding personality and its evolution. Jacobs claims that (1961). "The honor and merit of having revealed to observation dark abysses of the human mind rarely suspected before him" goes to Sigmund Freud.

"His theory has a scope, a unity, and a coherence that is unsurpassed in psychology," another psychologist, Inkless, has said. The personality theory of Sigmund Freud is a comprehensive theory that encompasses nearly all aspects of personality and its intricacies. It's a comprehensive approach to figuring out who you are.

Alfred Adler Theory: -

Adler was Freud's first follower, but he soon broke away from him and developed his own personality theory. In his philosophy, Adler places a high value on the goal, end goal, or meaning of one's life. "The final objective alone may explain man's behaviour," writes Adler in this context. Experiences, traumas, sexual development, and mechanisms cannot be explained, but the viewpoint in which they are viewed, the individual manner of perceiving them, which reduces all life to the ultimate objective, can."

Individual psychology is the name given to Adler's psychology since he emphasizes individual differences.

The major urge, according to Adler, is self-assertion rather than the sex impulse. Alfred's thesis downplayed the importance of sex, which Sigmund Freud had placed so much emphasis on. Adler believes that an individual's drive stems from social factors rather than just psychological ones. Every person aspires to create a distinct way of life in which sexual desire plays a minor role.

The major urge, according to Adler, is self-assertion rather than the sex impulse. Alfred's thesis downplayed the importance of sex, which Sigmund Freud had placed so much emphasis on. Adler believes that an individual's drive stems from social factors rather than just psychological ones. Every person aspires to create a distinct way of life in which sexual desire plays a minor role.

Consciousness, according to Adler, is the centre of personality. A self-aware individual is a self-aware individual. He is aware of his shortcomings and the objectives for which he strives.

Adler believes that childhood inadequacy is to blame for the development of feelings of inferiority in the first place. This sense of inadequacy stems from a perception of life's incompleteness or imperfection. It aids in the pursuit of greater levels of growth. Demosthenes, for example, was a stuttering child who grew up to be one of the world's finest orators. Similarly, President Roosevelt of the United States was a weeping in his childhood before becoming a physically powerful man through consistent training.

The way a person acts to overcome his feelings of inadequacy and gain feelings of superiority is shown by his way of living. There are numerous ways for a person to strive towards superiority. The basis by which an individual's personality functions is known as his or her style of living. Two aspects influence one's way of life: one's inner self and the forces of nature.

Early life experiences have a significant impact on a person's lifestyle. Adler believes that each person develops a self-structure based on his genetic makeup and the impressions he receives from his surroundings.

Carl Jung Theory: -

During the early days of psychoanalysis, Jung was a close friend of Sigmund Freud. He, like Adler, eventually disagreed with his mentor and established his own Analytical Psychology school. Jung believed that Freud's view of infantile sexuality was flawed.

Mental activity, according to Jung, takes four main forms: sensation, thinking, intuition, and feeling. Thinking and feeling are diametrically opposed, and both are always present in a person at the same time. If thinking is a person's primary mental activity, his or her unconscious tends to feel. Similarly, intuition and sensing are diametrically opposed.

There aren't many people who are outright extroverts or introverts. In general, people are a combination of the two. Most people exhibit traits of both introvert and extrovert personalities and are so classed as ambiverts.

Kurt Koffka: -

Koffka felt that most of the early learning is what he called "sensorimotor learning," or learning that occurs as a result of a consequence. A child who touches a hot stove, for example, will learn not to touch it again. Koffka also felt that a lot of learning happens through imitation, though he maintained that understanding how imitation works isn't important, just acknowledging that it happens naturally. The highest level of learning, according to Koffka, is ideational learning, which involves the use of language. Koffka points out that understanding that items have names is a critical stage in a child's development.

After participating in Wertheimer's phi phenomenon study, Koffka became interested in Gestalt psychology. Kurt Koffka worked at the Psychological Institute in Frankfurt in 1910 alongside Max Wertheimer and Wolfgang Köhler. They became the founding fathers of Gestalt psychology after focusing their research on sensory information and memory. Although Max Wertheimer is credited with inventing Gestalt psychology, Christian von Ehrenfeld's theory that a holistic melody is more than a simple arrangement of distinct sounds impacted them.

The Gestalt Principles were created in order to learn more about how the human eye perceives visual aspects. The concepts aid in understanding how complicated visual features can be broken down into simpler components. The principles also attempt to explain how the human eye perceives shapes as a single "object" rather than breaking them down into simpler components. Proximity, resemblance, and continuity were some of the most widely employed principles. The Gestalt concept of proximity states that visual elements that are near together are viewed as a totality.

Role of Family, Peer group and school in Adolescence
Introduction

Adolescence is a key period in a young person's life when it comes to their health and well-being. During this time, many young individuals are first introduced to psychoactive substances including alcohol, tobacco, and cannabis. One out of every five teenagers has a diagnosable mental health disorder. Mental health issues that begin in adolescence are associated with a tenfold higher long-term healthcare expense than those that begin in adulthood.

The Social Development Model has been widely used to explore the effects of micro-systems such as family and friends on young people's substance use (SDM). SDM proposes that social behaviors are acquired through social encounters, which result in the building of attachments that have a long-term impact on behavior by promoting the development of skills, norms, and values. Attachment to individuals who encourage and reward prosocial behavior protects against antisocial behavior, whereas attachment to those who encourage and reward antisocial behavior may increase risk behavior.

Family Relationship: -

Young people were asked about their family ties, including their impressions of how much essential matters were spoken, how much their family tries to help them, and how much emotional support they received. A component analysis revealed that items loaded onto two distinct factors, resulting in the creation of two distinct variables: one for family communication and the other for family (social and emotional) support, with Cronbach's alpha statistics of 0.86 and 0.95, respectively.

Mental Health of Adolescence: -

Young adults were asked to rate how frequently they felt down, irritable, anxious, or had trouble sleeping as part of a list of items used in previous international HBSC studies (Elgar et al., 2013) to evaluate mental health symptoms. All items had strong internal consistency when loading onto a single factor. This item was divided at the median to create a binary outcome variable due to the item's high degree of skewness.

Adjustment

The degree to which a person's personality successfully interacts with others is referred to as adjustment. It alludes to the harmonious interaction of an individual with their surroundings. In other terms, it refers to the interaction between organisms, their environment, and their personalities. A well-adjusted personality is well-equipped to fulfil the roles that are implied by the status that has been assigned to him in a particular setting. His demands will be met in accordance with societal requirements.

Adjustments as Process: -

The process of adjustment is crucial for psychologists, educators, and parents. We should examine a person's growth across time, starting at birth, in order to analyses the process. At birth, a child is totally reliant on others to meet his requirements, but as he gets older, he progressively learns to manage those demands. His interactions with his surrounding surroundings have a big impact on how well he adjusts. The universe is a great buzzing, flowering confusion when the child is born. He is unable to distinguish between the numerous items in his environment, but as he gets older, he develops the ability to verbalize the specifics of his surroundings through the processes of sensation, perception, and conceptualization.

Concept of Adjustment: -

The interaction that develops between a person and their environment is known as adjustment. Every person has a role to perform in their interpersonal relationships. He is taught to perform his duties in a way that meets all of his demands. As a result, he should fulfil his obligations fully. His requirements might not be met, and he might become irritated, if he does not do his duties in accordance with the guidelines and training acquired from Home Environment.

Adjustment Mechanism: -

"Any habitual strategy of overcoming blockages, accomplishing goals, satisfying reasons, relieving frustrations and maintaining equilibrium" may be used to define an adjustment mechanism. An adjustment mechanism is a tool used by people to lower their tension or anxiety so they may better adapt to their surroundings. It aids in his mental health recovery. A youngster may be protected from his frustrating situations if he employs particular self-adaptive, self-defensive strategies to manage his difficulties or deal with contradictory situations. We refer to these as defensive mechanisms. A youngster might be taught, for instance, to sleep through the night without requesting milk.

References: -

- https://www.indiastudychannel.comtypesofadjustment/
- https://link.springer.comroleoffamilypeergroupinadolescence
- https://www.verywellmind.compersonalitydefinitionconcept
- https://www.psychologydiscussion.net/psychology/theories-of-personality/

CHAPTER X

FOSTERING CREATIVITY AT WORKPLACE

Dr.Anshika Rajvanshi, Assistant Professor, Department of Management, IIMT, Delhi.

• • •

Introduction

"Creativity is seeing what everyone else has seen and thinking what no one else has thought." -Albert Einstein

The author believes that creativity is a collection of traits rather than a single trait. Intelligence, intense interest, knowledge, originality (ideas), creative instinct, nonconformity, courage, and persistence are basic elements of the concept of creativity. Creativity can manifest itself in a variety of areas of life, and at various stages, some of them are more prominent than others. The author tried to contribute the importance of Creativity at workplace which can result in significant works that benefit society as a whole and bring fame for the organization.

INTRODUCTION:

When we hear a word Creative we start thinking about different people who are involved in various creative tasks such as artist, painter, photographer, an author, may be a film maker or a chef or we start thinking of people who make things and we label them as creative type. But in reality there is no such word as creative type and every one of us is creative in some or the other aspects. Creativity can't be defined in one way but can be expressed differently. Creativity involves making things but it also involve mashing up ideas in different ways, it can mean thinking differently about data and finding unique solutions to varied practical problems, it can mean hacking system and tuning in different way, it can be exploring ideas and navigating information, it can mean designing system that empowers the creative work of others, it can mean creating change to the world and may be interaction with people etc. These approaches shape our work in a profound ways. The morale says that by looking at the creative side we should look out the creativity in ourselves.

The act of making new and imaginative ideas a reality is referred to as creativity. Creativity is defined as the ability to perceive the world in novel ways, to uncover hidden patterns, to connect seemingly unrelated phenomena, and to generate solutions. Creativity is comprised of two processes: thinking and producing.

A person is imaginative but not creative if he has ideas but do not act on them. Creativity is a combinatorial force: it is our ability to tap into our "inner" pool of resources – knowledge, insight, information, inspiration, and all the fragments populating our minds that we have accumulated over the years simply by being present, alive, and awake to the world, and to combine them in extraordinary new ways.

Components of Creativity:

There are two components for showing your creativity. One should have the courage to carry out it on a regular basis.

Originality: This aspect talks about that what so ever you have in your brain should be unique and not simply an extension of something else which already exist in the environment.

Functionality: This is related to that the idea must actually work or be useful in some way for the purpose it has generated.

Types of Creativity

Various Experts talked about various types of creativity. According to the "four c" model of creativity, there are four types:

"Mini-c" creativity entails personally meaningful ideas and insights known only to the self.

"Little-c" creativity is mostly concerned with everyday thinking and problem-solving. This type of creativity assists people in solving everyday problems and adapting to changing environments.

"Pro-C" Professionals who are skilled and creative in their respective fields engage in "Pro-C" creativity. These people are creative in their vocation or profession, but they do not achieve eminence for their work.

"Big-C" creativity entails producing works and ideas that are regarded as outstanding in their respective fields. This type of creativity leads to eminence and acclaim, and it frequently results in world-changing creations such as medical breakthroughs, technological advancements, and artistic accomplishments.

What it takes to be Creative: According to Csikszentmihalyi, creative people have a number of characteristics that contribute to their innovative thinking. Among these important characteristics are:

Energy: Creative people have an abundance of both physical and mental energy. They do, however, spend a lot of time quietly thinking and reflecting.

Intelligence: For many years, psychologists have believed that intelligence plays an important role in creativity. Researchers discovered in Terman's famous longitudinal study of gifted children that, while high IQ is required for great creativity, not all people with high IQs are creative. Csikszentmihalyi believes that creative people must be smart, but they must also be capable of seeing things in new ways, even if they are familiar.

Discipline: Creative people do not sit around waiting for inspiration. They are playful while also being disciplined in their pursuit of their work and passions.

While some people appear to be born with a natural gift for creativity, there are things you can do to improve your own. According to Csikszentmihalyi, creativity necessitates both a fresh perspective and discipline.

Creativity at workplace

Employees are more likely to collaborate when they are inspired to be creative. When they have new ideas, they seek feedback from colleagues. The creative process, by definition, encourages collaboration, and this is the most important advantage of providing a workplace conducive to creative thinking.

Now the question arises when does creativity happen at workplace? The answer of the question lies in itself and dependent on the willingness and positive attitude of a person to find out the solutions for the different problems.

Mihaly Csikszentmihalyi, a psychologist, suggested in his book Creativity: Flow and the Psychology of Discovery and Invention that creativity can be seen in a variety of situations.

When People are stimulating, interesting, and to have a wide range of unusual thoughts.

When People see the world through new eyes, have insightful ideas, and make significant personal discoveries.

When people achieve great creative accomplishments that are known throughout the world. The best example of this may include inventor Thomas Edison and artists Pablo Picasso.

When coming up with a solution to a problem, people with creative minds usually follow a process. This procedure frequently includes the following steps:

1. Planning and conducting research: This step involves gathering materials and conducting specific research on the task or problem at hand. You also conduct more general research on the subject and may employ more external information when problem-solving.

2. Problem-solving meditation: Instead of attempting to find a clear solution to the problem, begin to think deeply about it and experiment with various ideas that may eventually lead to a solution.

3. Disconnection from the issue: In this step, you take a long break from working on or thinking about the problem and potential solutions.

4. Allowing your idea to return to you: After fully removing yourself from the problem for a specified period of time, you will frequently gain new insight.

5. Developing and implementing the concept: Finally, you will be able to expand on your concept and apply it to your work. During this stage, you may want to consider sharing your idea with others to get feedback so that you can improve it further.

Benefits of Creative Workplace

Now day's companies are giving liberty to their employees to take part in Brainstorming sessions. They are also boost about being Innovative and creative but we are still way back in many of the aspects as creativity should be the continuous task in an organization. There may be few benefits which an organization may achieve by fostering creativity.

Better Team work and Team Building: Employees are more likely to collaborate when they are inspired to be creative. When they have new ideas, they seek feedback from colleagues. The creative process, by definition, encourages collaboration, and this is the most important advantage of providing a workplace conducive to creative thinking. Team bonding also contributes to employee engagement. Interactions are more likely among coworkers, even if they do not work together on a regular basis. A higher level of comfort in a team is beneficial to any organisation.

Improved Employee Attraction and Retention: Companies can attract more talented professionals by creating an environment that encourages creative thinking. They can fill positions in a more effective and efficient manner. Current employees experience a similar effect, as they are more likely to stay on board as a result of the creative environment. They become satisfied with their work and commit to it.

Problem-solving Abilities: The most important aspect of creativity, without a doubt, is how it affects the work. Employees who can think creatively and outside the box are more likely to come up with unique and innovative solutions to problems they face. This eagerness to solve problems can lead to novel approaches to completing tasks and running the organisation more efficiently.

Fostering creativity at work place

Creating the right working environment is critical for increasing employee productivity. This is based on scientific evidence. According to the study 'Happiness Works,' millennials expect to be happy at work and see their jobs as more of a valuable life experience than a paycheck.

Encourage both individualism and alliance: The strange thing about collaboration is that it necessitates both individuality and selflessness. Managers must not only encourage team bonding and collaborative work, but also ensure that employees' individuality is not checked at the door. Many unique ideas originate with a single person but are shaped by a team to become fully formed.

Never, Ever Say No: The brainstorming process can be delicate and complicated, particularly when a large team is working closely to find a strong solution. In these circumstances, it is all too easy to pass judgement on an idea and dismiss it as unsuitable. Rather than allowing negativity to stifle growth, promote positive and additive feedback. The phrase "yes and..." can go a long way toward assisting the entire team and they may associated with the organization for a long term.

Make Your Team More Diverse: To accelerate problem-solving, one simple and quick way to create a more creative workplace is to include a variety of perspectives, insights, and learning styles. The so-called Medici effect, proposed by author Frans Johansson, contends that diverse teams are more likely to generate innovative ideas due to the various approaches to a problem.

Encourage creativity in the workplace through Office Design: An inspiring work environment fosters creativity and innovation. Even if your office layout consists primarily of cubicles rather than open space, there are still ways to make employees feel inspired by their surroundings. You can, for example, encourage employees to bring in photos, prints, or small decorative items from home.

Allow for freedom and flexibility in how work is completed: Creativity in the workplace does not have to mean workplace creativity. A change of scenery can sometimes help spark new ideas. Change up your team's routine with off-site and walking meetings every now and then. Because it helps to break up the routine, brainstorming at a coffee shop may generate more ideas than you think.

Give people a voice — and follow through on good ideas: Whether anonymously or publicly, it is critical to ensure that people are heard and that they have opportunities to share feedback with one another in order to foster a culture of questioning and challenging ideas. After all, if people don't feel heard or have the opportunity to engage in dialogue, you're going to have a creative deficit in the workplace.

Recognize and reward creativity in the workplace: Recognizing a job well done is essential for keeping people engaged and motivated. And by recognising and rewarding individual and team engagement, you are more likely to be able to foster a creative work environment. As a result, when employees present an idea for a better way to solve a problem, complete a task, or even develop a new product or service, they are rewarded.

Brainstorm: In some ways, project management is nothing more than a never-ending attempt to boost corporate creativity. And brainstorming is a critical component of project management. That is because, as a project manager, you are constantly solving problems – and being creative about them – and, as Richard Branson says, two brains are simply better than one at doing so.

Change must be accommodated, and new technology must be embraced: Many people argue that technology fosters creativity. One of the reasons why technology may be beneficial to creativity is economic convenience. Technology allows you to test your ideas digitally before implementing them in real life, which saves you money and energy.

Provide your team with the appropriate tools (or suites) for creativity: The introduction of time and productivity tracking apps is one of the most recent trends in corporate work environments. The Pomodoro Technique was developed by Francisco Cirillo in the late 1980s to improve his productivity at university, but it has recently gained worldwide popularity.

Organizational Characteristics that Influencing Creativity

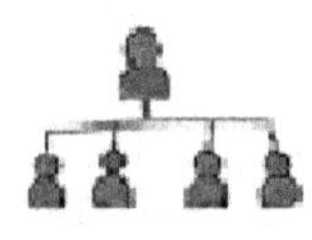

(Amabile, 1983)

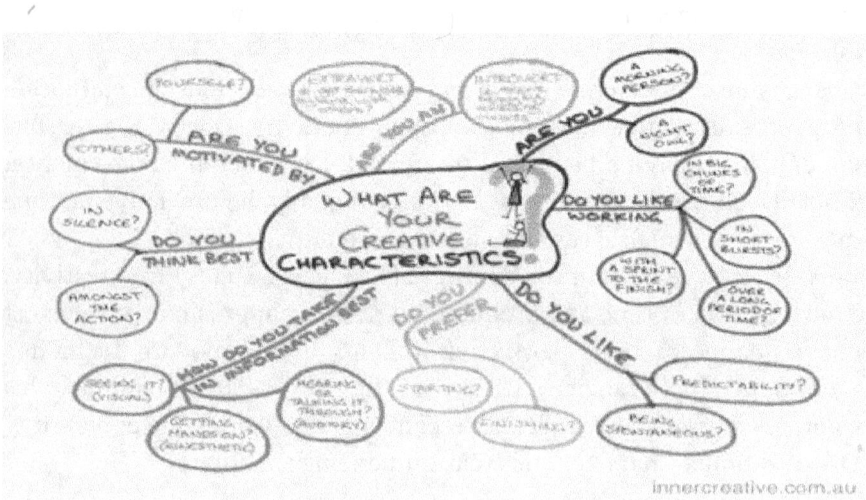

Check your Creative Characteristics

References:

- Amabile, T. M. (1983). The social psychology of creativity: A componential conceptualization. Journal of Personality and Social Psychology, 45(2), 357–376. https://doi.org/10.1037/0022-3514.45.2.357
- Amabile, T. M. (1983). The Social Psychology of Creativity. New York Springer-Verlag New York
- The science of creativity. American Psychological Association.
- Csikszentmihalyi M. Creativity: Flow and the Psychology of Discovery and Invention. New York: HarperCollins; 2013.\
- Kaufman J, Beghetto R. Beyond Big and Little: The Four C Model of Creativity. Review of General Psychology. 2009;13(1):1-12. doi:10.1037/a0013688
- Creativity https://www.csun.edu/~vcpsy00h/creativity/define.htm accessed on 28 June 2021
- Creativity at workplace https://www.creativityatwork.com/2014/02/17/what-is-creativity/ accessed on 28 June 2021.

CHAPTER XI

IVAN PAVLOV AND HIS DISCOVERY OF CLASSICAL CONDITIONING

Muskan Jindal, BA(Hons) Psychology, MA Psychology

• • •

Introduction

The learning theory of personality deals with the relationships between stimuli and responses. It falls under the behaviorism where observed behavior presents the model of personality. Behavioral psychology, commonly known as behaviorism, is a learning theory based on the concept that all behaviors are learned through conditioning. Personality, according to the behaviourist viewpoint, is nothing more (or less) than a set of learned behaviour patterns. They are unconcerned about the internal causes of behaviour. Personality is learnt by classical and operant conditioning, observational learning, reinforcement, extinction, generalization, and discrimination, much like any other learned behaviour. Strict behaviourists believed that anyone, regardless of genetic background, personality attributes, or interior thoughts, could theoretically be trained to execute any activity (within the limits of their physical capabilities). Only the proper conditioning is required.

The behavioural learning theory, sometimes known as behaviourism, is a popular notion that focuses on how individuals learn. All behaviours are taught through interaction with the environment, according to behaviourism. According to this learning theory, behaviours are acquired from their environment, and intrinsic or inherited characteristics have very little influence on behaviour.

Ivan Petrovich Pavlov (1849-1936) was born in Ryazan, Russia. He received the Nobel prize in 1904 for his work on the physiology of digestion. Pavlov was a skilled versatile surgeon who used dogs as experimental animals to create fistulas from various areas of the digestive tract, allowing him to get salivary gland, pancreas, and liver secretions without disrupting nerve and blood flow. Pavlov was a behaviourist who studied animal behaviour. This suggests that his beliefs were based on observable behaviour, as opposed to cognition, which cannot be quantified. Individual personality characteristics, according to Pavlov, are the outcome of learning and diverse contextual experiences. His theory is based on scientific data. Pavlov researched reflexes or automatic behaviours triggered by a stimulus in the environment. Some reflexes, such as blinking our eyes when a puff of air enters them or sucking a baby's mouth when something is placed in it, are learned. This automatic response can be influenced. This is referred to as conditioning. According to behavioural psychologists, there are two types of conditioning: classical and operant conditioning.

Classical conditioning

In order to study classical conditioning, Pavlov conducted an experiment. He chose his dog for this experiment. Pavlov began by performing a simple operation on his dog, inserting a rubber tube into the salivary gland to quantify the exact amount of saliva secreted during the trial. Following these preliminary steps, a neutral stimulus (e.g., a bell) was provided for a brief period of time, followed by a second stimulus known to induce salivation response and referred to as the unconditioned stimulus (e.g., Meat Powder). Conditioning trials were undertaken in quick succession, with each combination of the conditioned stimulus (CS) and unconditioned stimulus (UCS) serving as a conditioning trial. The CS (bell) developed the ability to elicit salivation as a result of repetitive matching. The conditioned response was named as the salivation to the bell (CR) began only after the training (CR). The salivation response to the meat powder, on the other hand, was called unconditioned response since it seemed to happen automatically (UCR).

CLASSICAL CONDITIONING

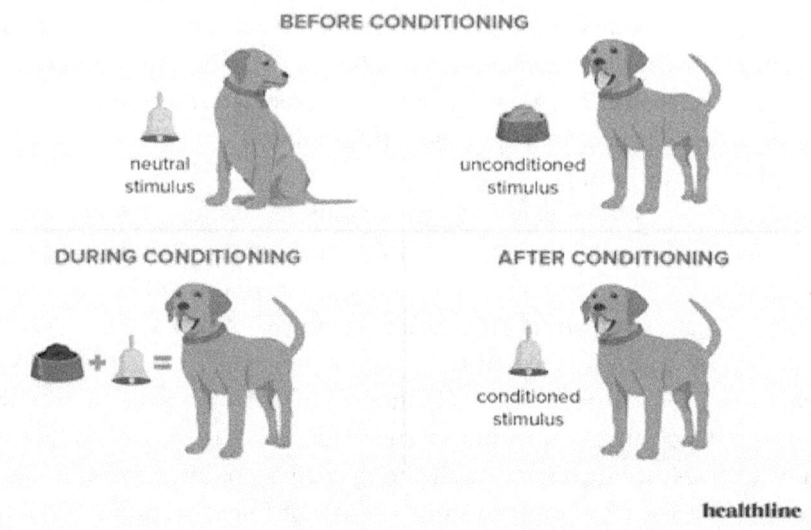

Source: Healthline

To understand the process of classical conditioning, it becomes important to study the stages of conditioning.

There are three phases of conditioning:

Phase1: Before conditioning (Learning)

A naturally occurring stimulus that will automatically elicit a response is required for the initial step of the classical conditioning process. A good example of a naturally occurring stimulus is salivation in reaction to the smell of food. The unconditioned stimulus (UCS) causes an unconditioned response during this stage of the process (UCR). When food is presented (the UCS), for example, a salivation reaction occurs naturally and automatically (the UCR).

Unconditional, natural, and automatic responses are elicited by an unconditioned stimulus. When you smell one of your favorite foods, for example, you may become quite hungry right away. The unconditioned stimulus in this case is the smell of the food. The unconditioned reaction is a natural response to an unconditioned stimulus that occurs without being taught. The unconditioned reaction in our case is a feeling of hunger in response to the smell of food.

Phase 2: During Conditioning

The previously neutral stimulus is repeatedly paired with the unconditioned stimulus during the second phase of the classical conditioning process. The previously neutral stimulus and the unconditioned stimulus create an association as a result of this pair.

Assume if when you smelled your favourite cuisine, you were also greeted by the sound of a whistle. While the whistle has little to do with the smell of the food, if it is repeatedly coupled with the fragrance, the whistle will eventually activate the conditioned reaction. The whistle's tone is the conditioned stimulus in this example.

Phase 3: After conditioning

Once the UCS and the CS have formed a relationship, providing the conditioned stimulus alone will elicit a response even if the unconditioned stimulus is not present. The conditioned response is the resultant response (CR). The learnt response to previously neutral stimuli is known as the conditioned response. The conditioned response in our scenario would be to feel hungry when you heard the whistle.

Principles of classical conditioning

Classical conditioning has been linked to a number of different occurrences, according to behaviourists. Some of these parts deal with the initial establishment of the response, while others deal with its extinction. Understanding the classical conditioning process requires an understanding of these factors

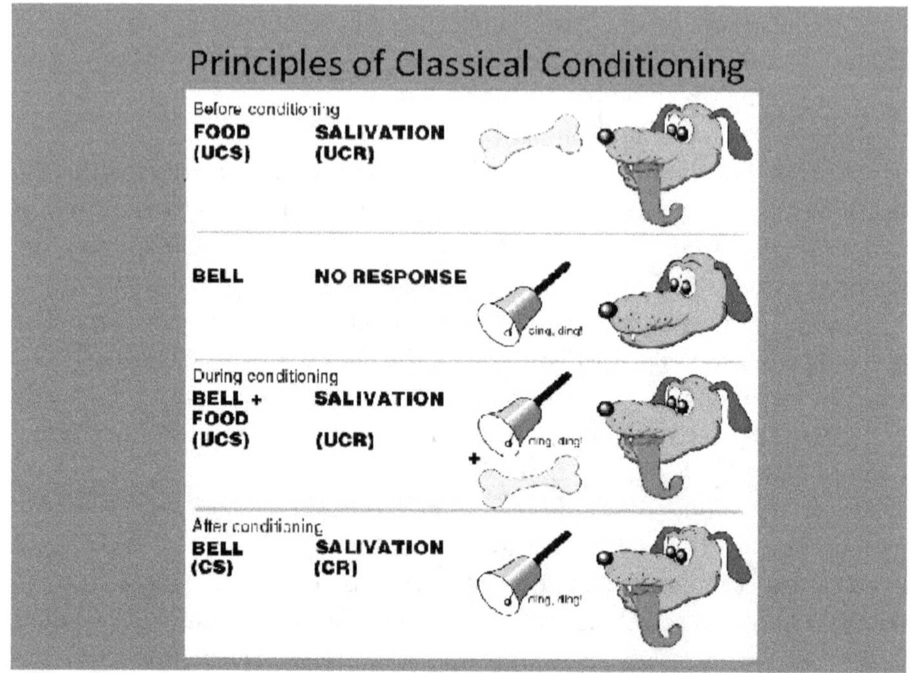

slidetodoc.com

Acquisition

The first stage of learning is acquisition, which is when a reaction is established and subsequently strengthened. A neutral stimulus is repeatedly associated with an unconditioned stimulus during the acquisition phase of classical conditioning.

The number of associations between this stimulus and the unconditioned stimulus is the first factor. As the number of pairings grows, the conditioned stimulus begins to elicit a stronger conditioned response. The size, latency, and likelihood of occurrence of the conditioned response are all used to determine the reaction's intensity. The interval that elapses between the presentation of the conditioned stimulus and the presentation of the unconditioned stimulus is the second factor that has a significant impact on the process of classical conditioning. Conditioning appears to be at its peak for a variety of responses when the interval is 0.50 seconds.

Consider the case of teaching a dog to salivate in response to the sound of a bell. You keep associating the sound of the bell with the appearance of food. When the dog begins to salivate in reaction to the bell tone, you can say the response has been acquired. You can gradually reinforce the salivation response once it has been established to ensure that the behaviour is well learnt.

Extinction

When the occurrences of a conditioned reaction decrease or cease, it is called extinction. This occurs when a conditioned stimulus is no longer paired with an unconditioned stimulus in classical conditioning. For example, if the smell of food (the unconditioned stimulus) was combined with the sound of a whistle (the conditioned stimulus), the conditioned response of hunger would be elicited. The conditioned response (hunger) would gradually fade if the unconditioned stimulus (the smell of food) was no longer associated with the conditioned stimulus (the whistle).

Spontaneous Recovery

Even after a period of extinction, a learnt reaction can resurface unexpectedly. The return of the conditioned response after a time of rest or reduced responsiveness is known as spontaneous recovery.

Take this example: after teaching a dog to salivate in reaction to the sound of a bell, you discontinue reinforcing the behaviour, and the response ultimately goes away. You abruptly ring the bell after a rest period during which the conditioned stimulus is not provided, and the animal spontaneously recovers the previously learned reaction.

After a spontaneous recovery, extinction will occur extremely quickly if the conditioned stimulus and unconditioned stimulus are no longer connected.

Applications of classical conditioning

The concepts of classical conditioning have been demonstrated to be extremely effective in changing behaviour. Classical conditioning concepts have also been used in the treatment of neurosis and phobias. Rather than focusing on the basis of the problem like a traditional psychopathologist, a behaviourist could use classical conditioning to eliminate the symptom. The psychopathological sickness of the patient could be cured by supporting the symptom's extinction. (Schwartz & Lacy, 1982).

Classic conditioning has also been demonstrated to be effective in the treatment of alcoholism and nicotine addiction. Addiction develops as a result of both the pleasurable physiological effects of nicotine and alcohol, which are unconditioned stimuli, and the taste of nicotine and alcohol, which are conditioned stimuli, according to Pavlovian principles. It is exceedingly easy to become addicted again when one quits swallowing the chemical, as in standard therapy approaches. After all, "simply not delivering a conditioned stimulus does not remove the relationship between it and unconditioned stimuli" (Schwartz & Lacy, 1982).

References

- Rouleau N, Karbowski LM, Persinger MA. Experimental evidence of classical conditioning and microscopic engrams in an electroconductive material. PLoS ONE. 2016;11(10):e0165269. doi:10.1371/journal.pone.0165269
- https://www.healthline.com/health/classical-conditioning
- Holland JG. Behaviorism: Part of the problem or part of the solution. J Appl Behav Anal. 1978;11(1):163-74. doi:10.1901/jaba.1978.11-163
- Morè L, Jensen G. Acquisition of conditioned responding in a multiple schedule depends on the reinforcement's temporal contingency with each stimulus. Learn Mem. 2014;21(5):258-62. doi: 10.1101/lm.034231.113
- Lattal KM, Lattal KA. Facets of Pavlovian and operant extinction. Behav Processes. 2012;90(1):1-8. doi:10.1016/j.beproc.2012.03.009
- Thanellou A, Green JT. Spontaneous recovery but not reinstatement of the extinguished conditioned eyeblink response in the rat. Behav Neurosci. 2011;125(4):613-25. doi:10.1037/a0023582
- Boulding, K. E. (1984). B. F. Skinner: A dissident view. Behavioural and Brain Sciences, 7, 483-484.
- Gracia, J., McGrown, B. K., & Green, K. F. (1972) Biological constraints on conditioning. In A. H. Black and W. F. Prokasy (Eds) Classical Conditioning II:Current Research and Theory. New York: Appleton-Century-Crofts.
- Rescorla, R. A. (1973). Pavlovlian conditioning: It's not what you think it is.American Psychologist, 43, 151-160.
- Schwartz, B., & Lacey, H. (1982). Behaviourism, science, and human nature.New York: Norton.
- Seligman, M. E. P. (1972). On the generality of the laws of learning. Psychological eview, 77, 406-418.

CHAPTER XII

A SPECTRUM OF JUNGIAN PSYCHOLOGY IN JHUMPA LAHIRI'S " INTERPRETER OF MALADIES"

Dr I. Saranya, Assistant Professor of English & IQAC Staff Coordinator, PG & Research Department of English, Thiagarajar College,(Affiliated to Madurai Kamaraj University), Madurai.

• • •

Introduction

Psychology is a broad discipline that studies the mind and behaviour of humans and animals. Human psychology encompasses the biological influences, social pressures and environmental factors, which affect the people's thought process. A Swiss psychologist and psychiatrist, Carl Gustav Jung was a sincere disciple of Sigmund Freud. He familiarized a few concepts like personality, archetypes and the collective unconscious in the stream of psychology. He had shown differences and new meanings to the same terms, which were popularized by Sigmund Freud. His works are influential in literature and religion. His main method in psychology is 'Analytic Psychology'. He analysed the psyche of his patients and found that it was the collective unconscious thoughts which they had inherited from their ancestors. He classified people into introvert and extrovert. People are classified based on these two types and play different 'Persona' in their lives. 'Persona' means an image of a human presented by him/her voluntarily in their respective social life. This social image is different from their private (personal) image. Jung also elaborated another term, Anima, which means the bisexual qualities present in humans. The present research article is elucidated on the Jungian psychology, which are applied in the select short stories of Jhumpa Lahiri. In many of the places, Male is arrogant, brutal, order-imposing, dominant and selfish creatures in the society. Jhumpa Lahiri's male characters are indifferent. Their characteristics, behavioural pattern and inner self reflect the Jungian Psychology.

Keywords: Psychology, Persona, Anima, Collective Unconscious, Introvert and Extrovert.

Humans and Non-humans are a part of universe. Both phenomenon do their roles, balance their lives and make the world sustainable. The more increasing demand of empowering the continents, countries, islands, nations and people, the more deteriorating the universe are also in progress. The advancement in the fields of education, science and technology has shrunken the world in one's palm. This tremendous growth of humans has resulted in their psycho-disorders. When their minds are disturbed and sick, it is cured by the psychiatrist. The psychiatrists are experts in psychology, which deals the mind and behaviour of the affected phenomenon. They have propounded many theories and applied the same and found the practical results.

Carl Gustav Jung, a Swiss psychologist, was a sincere disciple of Sigmund Freud. He elaborated on 'Analytical Psychology'. He further classified people into two types. The types were introvert and extrovert. He analysed the psyche of his patients and found that it was the collective unconscious thoughts which they had inherited from their ancestors. This research article is focussed on Jungian psychology applied in the select short stories from *Interpreter of Maladies* written by Jhumpa Lahiri.

Jhumpa Lahiri is an acclaimed writer. She has ancestral origin in India and is moved to America. Her stories portray cultural clashes and dilemmas of the main characters as the motif. It invariably presents the Indian characters and their double identity. Most of the characters in *Interpreter of Maladies* are Bengali, which symbolically represents the ancestry of Jhumpa Lahiri. The background, environmental factors and customs of Indians are also discussed in her works.

Interpreter of Maladies is a collection of nine short stories. The deeper reading of these stories reveals the characteristics and traumas of characters. Jhumpa Lahiri's characters battle hard to change their practices in the different cultural place like America. Her female characters are pondered over by many research scholars for their research works. Women are the kernel characters of Jhumpa Lahiri's stories. The textual study of women characters in *Interpreter of Maladies* visualizes their deep sorrows and inner conflicts. The male characters and their factual and fantasy world are not studied or researched properly by any of the research scholars. This article is intended to record the psyche of male characters in *Interpreter of Maladies* through Jungian psychology.

'Persona' is a term in Jungian psychology. It is a Latin word, means mask in ancient times. Humans exhibit their social face in their public life and hide their personal face. They pretend in society and hold the 'good impression' among others. Carl Gustav Jung referred this public image of man as social conscious mind, which is practised by them in their childhood itself. He referred the private image of man as unconscious mind. Unconscious mind is suppressed by individual purview of society.

In *Interpreter of Maladies*, Jhumpa Lahiri's male characters do hold their persona. Men are often associated with the qualities of arrogant, brutal, order-imposing, dominant and selfish. This is their persona. And they too have inner soft and delicate character in their unconscious mind. Jhumpa Lahiri's male characters also have tender unconscious mind, which is narrated to the readers in the stories.

Shukumar, in *A Temporary Matter*, is a scholar working on his dissertation on 'Agrarian revolts in India'. His wife is Shoba, a proof reader. They lead a silent and happy life. Shoba is calculative, good decision maker and plans ahead for future whereas Shukumar is a mediocre, silent and fragile character. When Shoba is pregnant and expecting the delivery, Shukumar has got an opportunity to attend an academic conference in Baltimore. He neglects the opportunity for Shoba, who could get labour at any time because the conference was just before three weeks of her due date. They lead a nuclear life; in turn none of their parents are with them to help Shoba in emergency. But Shoba insists him to undertake the journey, which would help him to get more contacts and job. She convinces him with the alternate arrangements through which she could manage in emergency.

"Six months ago, in September, Shukumar was at an academic conference in Baltimore when Shoba went into labor, three weeks before her due date. He hadn't wanted to go to the conference, but she had insisted; it was important to make contacts, and he would be entering the job market next year. She told him that she had his number at the hotel, and a copy of his schedule and flight numbers, and she had arranged with her friend Gillian for a ride to the hospital in the event of an emergency"(Lahiri 2, 3).

Shoba has undergone labour in the absence of Shukumar. The child is born dead. This incident distances them. Shoba and Shukumar have become silent partners of their house. They have stopped their communication except during the dinner. Shoba has resumed her work as proof reader. Shukumar couldn't continue his teaching as well the dissertation. He prefers to stay at home and cooks dinner for them.

Language is a tool of communication. When people stop communicating each other, there the problem rises. The myriad gap happens between the relationship of Shoba and Shukumar, when they have stopped communicating each other. Shukumar is silently mourning for the death of their child. He couldn't concentrate on any other works. He doesn't have the courage to look at Shoba. He rises from the bed at late by the time Shoba would have left the home for work. "These days Shoba was always gone by the time Shukumar woke up...it was often nearly lunchtime when Shukumar would finally pull himself out of bed and head downstairs to the coffeepot"(4,5).

Shoba and Shukumar have become experts in avoiding each other. They receive information about electricity cut for five days nearly an hour, beginning at 8:00PM. This darkness provides them the platform to share their innermost self to another one. Each time Shukumar looks at Shoba, he is reminded of the pregnant image of Shoba. "Each time he thought of that moment, the last moment he saw Shoba pregnant, it was the cab he remembered most, a station wagon, painted red with blue lettering"(3).

Shoba starts the game of revealing the truth, which they have concealed so far from each other. They get united in this game. At the fifth day, Shoba tells that she has the plan to vacate the house. She needs to be alone for some time. Shukumar reveals the truth that their baby is a boy and so pinkish, which he has planned to keep that as secret from Shoba in their remaining married life. He holds the boy until the nurse gets the child from him.

"Our bay was a boy," he said."His skin was more red than brown. He had black hair on his head. He weighed almost five pounds. His fingers were curled shut, just like yours in the night"(22).

Shukumar's unconscious mind is naïve and has pure love for his wife. Everybody believes that Shukumar arrived to the hospital much late. That is not true. Shukumar had been in the hospital early. After revealing this, both of them moan for their child's death. Shukumar is a man who loves his wife the most and even though he doesn't like to have a child, when he is still a student as well he doesn't hate also. Many instances he admires the inbuilt skills of his wife, Shoba.

Kapasi, in *Interpreter of Maladies*, is a travel guide, driver and interpreter. He is a well-educated man to the social world. He is a middle class man, who strives to achieve success in his career. He is a polyglot and knows nine languages. He expects to be become an Ombudsman or ambassador whereas he has ended his life in doing menial jobs. He does his profession without interest.

"The job was a sign of his failings. In his youth he'd been a devoted scholar of foreign languages, the owner of an impressive collection of dictionaries. He had dreamed of being an interpreter for diplomats and dignitaries, resolving conflicts between people and nations, settling disputes of which he alone could understand both sides" (52).

Neither the society nor the family appreciates his skills. He renews his interest in his profession through Mrs. Das, a foreigner and mother of three kids, who appreciate his job. Mrs. Das enquires about his interpreter profession in hospital and wonders at him. Mrs. Das explains him that the interpreter in hospital is a great profession and the patients need him the most than the doctor. Mr.Kapasi's personal life is so weird. He keeps himself occupied in his professions in all the days to forget his professional failure. He considers his interpreter profession as a thankless profession. When Mrs. Das explains him the importance of his profession, he realizes its significance.

Man expects a mark of appreciation for his completed tasks. Mr. Kapasi's conscious mind (persona) is a gentle, well-learned man, fulfilling father and husband. His unconscious mind has sexual notion and dominant nature. When Mrs. Das addresses his profession as romantic, his mind is intoxicated. He develops a sexual interest in Mrs. Das, who is in the age of his daughter. He compares his marriage life with hers and decides both of the couple is bad match. His unconscious mind intrudes in the personal life of Mr. Das and Mrs. Das.

Mr. Kapasi has noticed the strange behaviour of Mr. Das and Mrs. Das, who scheduled their role as parents. The traditional Indian parenting is emotional whereas the western parenting is more logical and liberal. His subconscious mind devours the half-dressed woman in the tourism spots, the topless women in the Sun Temple at Konark and compares it with his own wife, who hasn't rendered those looks. This amorous nature of Mr. Das is explicitly mentioned in the following lines:

"...it occurred to him, as he, too, gazed at the topless women, that he had never seen his own wife fully naked. Even when they had made love she kept the panels of her blouse hooked together, the sting of her petticoat knotted around her waist. He had never admired the backs of his wife's legs the way he now admired those of Mrs. Das, walking as if for his benefit alone" (58).

Shukumar and Mr. Das are the most literate characters in *Interpreter of Maladies*, a short story collection of Jhumpa Lahiri. Shukumar's conscious mind and subconscious mind is naïve and full of love for his wife and expresses the same to her at the end. They reconcile each other. Even though Shukumar is selfish and dislikes his wife, Shoba, he constantly admires the qualities of her. Whereas Mr. Das's conscious mind is decent and genuine, his unconscious mind proves his true colour, amorous and dominant character. Jhumpa Lahiri is a forceful writer, who envisages the society better to her readers.

Bibliography

- Barry, Peter. *Beginning theory: An Introduction to literary and cultural theory. Second edition.* Viva Books pvt ltd, 2008.
- Crystal, David. *Language Death.* Cambridge University, 2010.
- Krishnaswamy, N, John Varghese, and Sunita Mishra. *Contemporary Literary Theory: A Student's Companion.* Macmillan, 2001.
- Lahiri, Jhumpa. *Interpreter of Maladies Stories.* Harper Collins, 2002.

CHAPTER XIII

FREUD'S PSYCHOANALYTIC THEORY ON PERSONALITY

Gurpinder Kumar, Assistant Professor, Centre for Women's Studies, University of Allahabad, Prayagraj, UP-211002, INDIA.

• • •

INTRODUCTION

Freud's psychoanalytic theory, personality develops in stages, each of which is characterized by a certain degree of internal mental conflict. Sigmund Freud ' s psychoanalytic theory of personality argues that human behavior is the result of the interaction of the three parts of the mind: the id, ego and super-ego. This theory is known as Freud's structural theory of personality, which is strongly focused on the role of unconscious psychological conflicts in shaping behavior and personality. The dynamic interactions between the key components of the mind are thought to develop through the use of five different psychosexual stages of development. However, in the last century, Freud's ideas have been the subject of criticism, in part because of his emphasis on sexuality as the most important driver of the development of one's personality. According to Freud, our personality develops as a result of interaction between what is offered in the three most important structures of the human mind: the id, ego and super-ego. The conflict between these three structures, and we strive to have a balance between all of those "desires" to determine how we are to conduct ourselves and how we relate to the world. How do we achieve balance in a given situation, determine how to resolve the conflict between the two different behavioral tendencies; our biological aggressive and pleasure-seeking drives vs. our socialized internal control over those drives.

erywellmind.com

The Id

The Id is the most primitive of the three structures, is concerned with instant gratification of basic physical needs, and motivations. It works in a completely unconscious (without consciously having to think). For example, if you're ID walked past by a stranger consuming ice cream, then, most likely, to have this for itself. It doesn't know, or care, that it would be impolite to accept something that someone else; you are only interested in having that ice cream.

Super-ego

Super-ego is in related to the social principles and moral values which is similar to what a lot of people say it is known as "moral compass". It develops as the child learns what is good and what is bad in the part of their culture. If you're super-ego is passed through the same, or a stranger, he should take out for ice cream, because you knew that it would be rude. However, if you have the id and super-ego are involved, and id be strong enough to overcome your super-ego's fears, on the ice, but after that, you would most likely feel guilty and ashamed for your actions.

The Ego

In distinction to the instinctual id and the moral superego, and the ego is the rational, pragmatic part of our personality. It is less primitive than the id and is partly conscious and partly unconscious. This is what Freud believed that the self and the goal are to balance the demands of the id and the super-ego, in the practical context of the real thing. So, if you walked past the stranger with ice-cream, and your ego is to mediate the conflict between the id (I want to have that ice cream cone now) and the superego (It is wrong to take other people's ice cream), and you decided to buy their own. While this may mean that you will have to wait another 10 minutes, which will hinder your id, your ego, and superego decides to make that sacrifice, as part of a compromise to satisfy his desire for ice cream, or avoidance of an unpleasant social situation, and the potential embarrassment. Freud believed that the id, ego, and superego are in constant conflict, and that adult personality and behavior has its roots in the outcome of this internal conflict during childhood. He believed that a person who has a strong ego, a person, a sound, and a disturbance in the system can lead to neurosis (what we now call anxiety and depression, and unhealthy behaviors.

Freud's Theory of Development

1. What is Freud's Psychoanalytic Theory of Development? Freud believed that there are five stages of psychosexual development:
2. Oral (from birth to one year of age)- the period when the Id asserts itself through oral behaviors driven by the libido and leading to future habits: sucking the thumb, biting the fingernails, and smoking.
3. Anal (ages 1-3)- behavior is centered on the anus through defecation and asserted by the Ego; toilet training techniques may lead to obstinacy, obsessive neatness, swearing, stubbornness, and issues with authority.
4. Phallic (ages 3-6)- due to the Oedipus Complex, the libido revolves around the genitals and may lead to jealousy, fears of rejection, and erotic attractions.
5. Latency (ages 6-puberty)- the Ego and the Superego are active during this passive period, ushering in thoughts and behaviors that channel sexual energy into friends, hobbies, and studies.
6. Genital (puberty-adulthood)- the Superego reigns during this time of sharing sexual pleasure with others, developing sexual perversions, and discovering the right sexual partner.

Psychosexual stages of development

Freud believed that the nature of the conflict between the id, ego and super-ego, changes over time, if a person is changing from a child to an adult. In particular, he argues that such conflicts have to go through a series of stages, each with a different sexual orientation: oral, anal, phallic, latent, and genital. He referred to the idea that the psychosexual theory of development, in which each of the psychosexual stage, which is directly related to the physical center of the fun. Freud's theory of psychosexual development comprises five stages. According to Freud, each stage is carried out in a period of your life. If a person is preoccupied in each of the four stages, he or she develops a personality, according to a certain stage, and the focus. The first stage, the oral stage. The baby at this stage is from birth to eighteen months. The oral phase is focused on the pursuit of pleasure, from the mouth of the baby. At this stage the need for the testing and the related vacuum, visible to the fun. Oral stimulation and it is of paramount importance at this stage as to meet the needs of the child are not met during this time period; the focus will be on the oral stage. A fixation at this stage can result in an adult's habits, such as thumb sucking, smoking, eating too much, and a nail biting. At your age, personal characteristics, are associated with the oral fixation may also occur; these characteristics are optimism, and independence, or the pessimism and hostility. The second stage is the anal stage, which lasts from eighteen months to three years. At this stage, the child's pleasure-seeking centres are located in the intestines, and bladder. During this period, the parents are to pay special attention to the potty training and bowel control. The fixation at the anal stage might lead to anal retentive. Anal retentive characteristics include excessive conscientiousness, accuracy, and good order, while the anal ban is going to disorganization, disorder, and destruction. The third stage is the phallic stage. It begins at the age of three years old, and lasts for up to six. Now the sensitivity is focused on the genitals, masturbation (for both sexes) is a new source of pleasure. The child will begin to understand the anatomical differences between men and women, which have led to a sense of jealousy and fear, which Freud called the Oedipus complex (in boys). Later, the Freudian scholars are added to the Electra complex (in girls). The fourth stage is that of the secret place, starting at the age of six, and it will run until the end, but maybe not. At this stage, not a single part of your body and looking to have fun instead of all of the sexual feelings are repressed. In this way, children can develop social skills, and comfort in social interactions with peers and family members. In the final stage of psychosexual development is the genital stage. This stage begins at the age of eleven, and continues up to the age of puberty, and ends when a person reaches adulthood at the age of eighteen years of age. The onset of puberty, which reflects a person's strong interest in a person to other opposite sexes. If a person does not have experience with the consent of the psychosexual stages, the reach of the genital stage, they will have a well-balanced person.

Criticism of Freud's theory

Even though Freud's theories have a number of advantages that have contributed to the expansion of our psychological understanding of personality, and they are not open-ended. The focus is on the structure of human consciousness, Freud's little attention has been paid to the influence of the environment, the social sciences or the world. His theories were strongly committed to the region, and to a large extent ignored the "normal" healthy effect. He has also been criticized for his narrow minded attitude to human sexuality, to the exclusion of other important factors. Many critics point out that Freud's theories are not supported by the empirical (experimental) evidence. In fact, when scientists began to examine his ideas of a more scientifically, it has become clear that some of them could not be confirmed that a theory is scientific, it needs to be able to rule out ("forge"), as well as the experimental evidence, and many of Freud's ideas are not falsifiable. It is worth pointing out, and contemporary critics have been very critical of many of Freud's theories, which seems to indicate that the accounting policies and methods of psychoanalytic theory, is deeply patriarchal (male-dominated), and anti-feminist, and misogynistic (anti-women). Karen Horney, a psychologist, traveled to Freud, they believed that the "Freudian approach as a foundation, "the male one." Feminist Betty Friedan referred to Freud's concept of penis envy" is purely a social bias that is typical of the Victorian era, and demonstrates how this concept played a crucial role in discrediting alternative ideas regarding the female in the beginning and in the middle of the twenty-first century.

Neo-Freudian approaches to personality

Even though Sigmund Freud was an important contribution to the field of psychology, it is thanks to his psychoanalytic theory of personality; his work was not well studied. Many people have made criticisms of his theories, the focus is on issues of sexuality; and, in the years that have passed, it is his work, and many, many other researchers have tweaked and developed his ideas for the creation of a new theory of the personality. This is the neo-Freudian theorists generally agreed with Freud that childhood experiences were important, but they have reduced the emphasis on sex and sexuality. Instead of a strictly biological approach to the development of personality, such as Freud did, by focusing on the individual, the evolutionary gestures), they focus more holistically on how the social context and culture impact on the individual's development. A lot of psychologists, scientists, and philosophers have made significant additions to the psychoanalytic studies of the personality. The four most well-known neo-Freudians include Alfred Adler, Erik Erikson, Carl Jung and Karen Horney.

Neo-Freudian Personality Theory

- Social relationships are fundamental to formation and development of personality.
- **Alfred Adler:**
  - People seek to attain rational goals in life (Style of life) and;
  - Reduce Feelings of inferiority by striving for superiority.
- **Harry Stack Sullivan**
  - We continuously establish significant and rewarding relationships with others to reduce tensions such as anxiety.
- **Karen Horney's three personality groups**
  - Compliant: move toward others. A compliant individual desires to be loved, wanted and appreciated.
  - Aggressive: move against others. aggressive individual desires to excel and win admirations.
  - Detached: move away from others. detached person desires independence, self reliance and freedom from obligation.

Study: highly compliant students prefer name-brand products like Bayer. Aggressive students prefer masculine appeal brands like Old Spice.. Whereas detached proved to be heavy tea drinkers as a sign of difference.

slidetodoc.com

Alfred Adler

Alfred Adler was the first to explore the development of a comprehensive social, psychodynamic theory of personality. He founded a school of psychology called individual psychology, which focuses on what we need to do in order to compensate for feelings of inferiority. Adler introduced the concept of the inferiority complex, that is, how a person's feelings that they don't matter, and does not conform to the standards of others or of the community. He, too, believed in the importance of social relations, in view of the fact that the child will be considered during the development of the social development, on the site of the sexual phase, described by Freud. On the basis of these ideas, Amenities and identifies three important tasks that all of us have to solve are: occupational tasks (careers), social (friendship), and love tasks (such as finding a partner for a long-term relationship.

Eric Erickson

Erik Erikson is best-known for the proposal of the psycho-social theory of development, in which it is assumed that a person's personality develops over a lifetime, on the basis of social relationships, and a departure from Freud's biology is focused on the view. In his psychological theory, Erickson emphasized the social relationships, which is the case in each of the stages of development of the personality, in contrast to Freud, who stresses the need to have sex. Erickson has identified eight stages, each of which is a dispute or a challenge. The development of a healthy personality and a sense of competence are subject to the successful completion of each task.

Carl Jung

Carl Jung is followed by Adler's footsteps, to the development of a theory of personality, in which analytical psychology, it is concerned. One of Jung's most important contributions was the concept of the collective unconscious, which he regarded as Freud's, as the "universal" version of the personal unconscious mental patterns, or memory traces, which are common to all of us (Jung, 1928). These ancestral memories, which, Jungian archetypes, are represented by the universal themes expressed in terms of the art and literature of the different cultures, as well as the dreams of the people. Jung introduced the concept of the persona, which refers to a kind of "mask" that is what we have on the basis of our experience, and in this course, as it is in our collective unconscious. Jung believed that the person is acting as a trade-off between who we really are (our true self) and the society expect from us; we hide behind a mask, which can be the parts of ourselves that do not meet up to the expectations of the society.

Karen Horney

Karen Horney was one of the first women to be trained as a Freudian psychoanalyst. Karen Horney's theories have focused on the "unconscious anxiety", which, she believed, came from the early childhood experiences, needs and challenges, of loneliness and / or isolation. Karen theorized the three styles of coping that they take in relation to fear of movement in the direction of people, moving away from the people and for the movement of people. Karen Horney was also a major influence on the development of feminism in the field of psychodynamics. To Freud, it is often criticized for the installation of almost all men for what some see as a retreat for the women; for example, Horney disagreed with the Freudian idea that the girls are jealous of the penis, and is jealous of the men of biological functions. According to Horney, each and every blind is the most likely to the level of permissions that are often people who have it, which means that the differences between men's and women's personalities emerge from the dynamics of culture, not of biology. Furthermore, it suggests that men experience womb envy" because they don't have.

Gender-based socialization

One way to interpret that Beauvoir's declaration of a person is not born, but becomes, a woman has to take it as an indication of the socialization of gender, females become women, and the processes by which they are acquiring female characteristics, and learn how women's behavior. It is believed that masculinity and femininity is the product of the nurse or the nursing units. They may be causally structured (Haslanger, 1995), social forces have a main playing role in the development of the gender of the individuals, and (in some sense) to shape the way in which they become, women, and men. The mechanism of the activities of social learning. For example, Kate Millett, is of the opinion that the gender differences between men and women above all, the cultural rather than the biological foundation, which is the result of a variety of relationships, (Millet, 1971). For her, gender is the fullness of your parents, peers, and culture, the perception of what is appropriate for one's gender, temperament, personality, interests, status, dignity, a gesture and a word (Millett 1971). Male-and-female-gender-norms, however, are a problem in the generation of behavior that fits comfortably in the subordination of women, and to ensure that women are socialized in a subordinate role in society, they are taught to be passive, ignorant, easy-going, emotional, machines for men. However, because these roles are to be taken into account, we can create a more equal society, and "unlearning" of social roles. That is, women should aim to reduce the impact of socialization. Social learning theorists believe that there are such a lot of different influences that is to socialize us, women as well as men. In this case, it's very hard to stand up to gender socialization. For example, parents are often unaware of the treatment for male and female children differently. When parents were asked to describe it, it is available 24 hours a day for the kids, and they were, therefore, the use of gender-stereotyped language, the boys are described as strong, alert, and in a consistent manner, and the girls are described as " a small, soft, and tender. Parents ' attitudes toward their children will also give the descriptions, whether they are aware of it or not (Renzetti & Curran 1992). Some of socialization, it is even more pronounced: the children are often dressed up in a sex-stereotyped clothing and colors, the boys are dressed in blue and girls in pink, and the parents tend to buy their children's gender-stereotyped toys and games. They also have the tendency to (intentionally or not), and to strengthen some of the "good" behavior. Although the precise form of the socialization of the sexes has changed a lot since the arrival of the second wave of feminism, and even today, girls are not encouraged to play sports, such as football, or playing the "rough and tumble" of the game, and they are more likely than boys to the doll or other accessories, toys to play-the boys are told not to "cry like a baby" and give men's toys such as cars and guns. According to the theories of social learning, children will also have an impact on what we see in the world. This makes it more difficult to counter gender socialization. First of all, in the books of the children, men and women are represented in real life stereotypes, for example, men, women, and leaders, as well as the women's assistant and the students. One of the best ways to deal with gender stereotyping in children's books, and was the portrayal of women in an independent role, while the men were not aggressive, and health care (Renzetti & Curran 1992). Some publishers have attempted to use an alternative approach, which makes their characters-for example, gender neutral, animals, or asexual imaginary creatures, (such as the teletubbies on TV). However, the parents in the book, of gender-neutral or genderless characters are often undermining the publishers of the efforts made by them to read with their children in such a way that the characters are either male or female. According to Renzetti and Curran, parents are called, and the vast majority of those are gender-neutral, male characters, such as characters, that are compatible with the female gender stereotypes (such as good) and were referred to as a woman (Renzetti & Curran, 1992). The interacting effects of these are thought to have implicit messages about how men and women should behave, and it is expected that you will work through us, created in both female and male personalities.

Psychoanalytic feminism

Psychoanalytic feminism is the theory of grief, which states that men have a psychological need to submit to women. The roots of the men's desire for dominance over women, and women with the minimum of resistance, and the submission to lie deep within the human psyche. This branch of feminism that strives to gain knowledge about how the life of a reason to evolve in order to better understands it and to change it, the oppression of women. The model reduction is also integrated in the society, and the creation and maintenance of patriarchy. With the help of psychoanalytic methods in order to examine the differences between men and women, as well as ways to build the gender, you can reorganize the socialization of the models are in the early stages of the human life. Social change or "cure" may be made by the open-source of the complete dominance in the male psyche, and submission of the female psyche and that is largely unnoticed, in the ignorance of the people.

Psychoanalysis and feminism

"The Second Sex" by Simon de Beauvoir (1949), and "The Feminine Mystique" by Betty Friedan (1963), both theorized psychoanalysis as stated women as being inferior, and defined only in relation to men. Then, in the 1970s, a second wave of feminist works, such as Kate Millet's Sexual Politics (1970) The Dialectic of Sex by Shulamith Firestone (1970), and Germaine Greer's The Female Eunuch (1970), has called for changes in the society, which is helping to tackle sexual inequality. Mitchell's book, Psychoanalysis and Feminism (1972), was an important milestone in the revival of the analysis, and the interpretation of the revolutionary concept of the women. As of the start of the analysis, the argument is that the physical reality of the race is to be distinguished from the anatomical fact, that there is no clear correlation between the fields of biology and psychology. Men and women have been physically or socially "made" as men or the women, but they become such. Initially, however, as Freud assumed, a symmetry in the development of what he called the Oedipus complex. Alone, in an essay written in 1925, it was for Freud, a distinction should be made between the psychosexual history of the boys and girls, and recognizing the importance of the pre-oedipal phase, in which the boys and girls, for the love of the mother, and the two have to abandon her in favor of the father (1925). A young girl with the love of her mother, her father, and it is as if a man wants to be a mother, in the sense that, later on, his wife. In this model, the boys identify with their fathers, and because of their masculine identity are determined. A boy learns of his role as a father, the heir. The girl, on the other hand, has to be able to identify with the mother, while at the same time, a rejection of her as an object of love, the love, object and turning to her father instead.

According to Freud, the date of the rejection by the mother, it is based on the frustration, and the frustration that is not able to meet her mother's, and it goes hand in hand with the enemy. The importance of pre oedipal relationship a mother has been fully discussed, since Freud's time. Recently, interest in the nature of a female's personality is reflected in the works of Ethel Guy, Irene, Soon, and Jessica Benjamin, and in the United States, as well as in the work of Janine Chasseguet-Smirgel, Catherine J., and Jean-Parat, Marie, and Toroc, and Joyce McDougall in France. In the 1920's, a controversy broke out on the perception of femininity. If Freud's libido, it is the same for both sexes; it is, in the English language school by the female sex drive is. Karen Horney and Ernest Jones who took part in a series of exchanges, and argued against Freud's view of the making of a "positive" image of women's sexuality is distinct from the concept of the provision of services. For Jones, the evolution of the female is associated with a physical constitution. In a legal dispute with him, as well as Freud pointed out that he deeply understood the basic nature of the sexuality, and that he had been restored to the biological reductionism. Mitchell said that, in the Freud - Jones, the controversy has shifted to the question of the differences between men and women, on what is specific to each gender. The development of the psychoanalytic theory in the UK, along with the school of objects relations, and lead to a focus on the parent-child dyad and the role of motherhood. Psychoanalytic work from the early focusing on the poor conditions in the early stages, and gradually, the attention is focused on the impact of the poor conditions at the time of transfer. Melanie Klein's theory continued to Freud, the shift of emphasis from the father, the mother, and the importance of a mother to the children of both sexes. In front of her, and the relationship of the child to the mother's body has been described above, the emotional life. In particular, the breast is a ratio; it is of crucial importance in a child's early experiences. Klein's concept of the instructive, and projective identification, are metaphors for the body of the processes of the absorption of the movement. According to Klein, it's a little girl who believes that her mother's body has everything it needs, including those of her father's penis. The result of this is a girl who is full of hatred for her mother, and wants to attack you and rob you of the inside of the body. After that, she filled out due to the fear of being "having the inside of her body robbed and destroyed." In 1928, the Small, pointed out that it is in the chest, discomfort, and it is not the discovery of the lack of a penis, the girl away from her mother to her father.

Later on, she played down the child of the first one breast, jealousy, envy, and he wrote specifically about heterosexual attraction to young girls. A small view of the early mother-child relationship, and the effect of some earlier work on the subject of femininity in society, more reasonable approach is to start with the investment by the funds in advance so that you are prepared for the purpose. Progressive psychoanalysts from all sections of British society, and was inspired by the work of Klein, Donald Winnicott, Marjorie Brierly, and Wilfred Bion, which emphasizes the connection between the primary emotional development, and object relationships. These patterns can be found in the writings of Marion Burgner Pink and Adcumbe, Aigle Laufer, Dinora Pines, Said Brin, Joan Raphael-Leff, and Rosina Perelberg. In a later collection, this is found in the work of the three schools of psycho-analysis in the British Psychoanalytical Society, and Raphael-Leff, and Perelberg emphasis primal connection to the mother, and for her appearances in the transference and counter transference. American feminists believe that the analysis provides a patriarchal inequality. Nancy Chodorrow is one of the best-known writers in the United States, on the connection between psycho-analysis and feminism. The Reproduction of Mothering: Psychoanalysis and the Sociology of Gender (1978) introduced American readers to the work of the Winnicott, W. Ronald Fairbairn, and Harry Gantrip. Chodorow stresses on development in relation to the others, with a focus on the pre-Oedipal relationship between mother and child. They will have the function of being a mother to an asymmetric relationship between the boys and the girls. Girl has more permeable boundaries in your relationships with others and, as a result of the fact that she's a mother, a person of the same sex. Why do girls and women are more devoted to being a mother. The boys, on the contrary, they will develop a sense of self-esteem, in contrast to the mother, and to set more stringent limits. Men's perceptions of themselves are more spread out. Jean Baker Miller, and Carol Gilligan, of the School of inter-personal Analysis to emphasize the feminine traits of a relationship, moved to pity, and to make sure that it can be considered to be a decline in a male-dominated culture. These interpersonal theorists emphasize the cultural focus on the different characteristics of men and women, and the focus is less on the inner world of unconscious fantasies, and the internal object relations. Jessica Benjamin in the "Bond of Love" (1988) and, see both, boys, and girls looking for their father, and to confirm it. While the boy's identity is confirmed by the father, the girl in contrast has her identification with the father's power denied, and he becomes the object of her ideal ego. This will prevent her from having a "will of its own, and her desire for her father to be tinge with masochism, issues of power and submission in the sphere of relationships. Chodorow, the argument is that what all these authors have in common, despite their differences, the strain on their sites as "not applicable" (or the non-acceptance of the relationship). She argues that this position is an abrupt break with the essentialist view of gender, and is moving in the direction of the view that, by default, masculinity and femininity, in order relationally constructed context. These schools, but in the end, the building of a more stable view of femininity and masculinity than Earlier, which is, in principle, to the fact that there is a flow between masculinity and femininity in both men and women. These features can be compared with the latest trends in the French theories of psychoanalysis, and feminism, which is to emphasize unconscious fantasies, and desires, and try to find a language for the expression of the feminine principle. Below are the French psychoanalysts, in particular, there is an opinion that the "discovery" of the unconscious is, in itself, does not reveal the fact that the person is in a state of fantasy and desire. This is a radical perspective in the analysis can provide with feminism. The impact of the work of Jacques Lacan, permeates much of the work of those who accept the postulates of Freudian theory, and to those who, like Julia Kristeva, Helene Sixus, Michel Montreulet, Sarah Kofman, and Luce Irigaray continued to be very critical for the analysis of the basic assumptions. Lacan pointed out, that is, the difference between the penis and the phallus, it is fundamental to Freud's distinction between the biological and psychological reality. The phallus is the anatomical reality; it is a symbol of the mother's desire. Joel Dor suggested that the central question of the Oedipus complex, and it is, therefore, "to be or not to be the phallus," which is to say, to be or not to be to the object of her desire. The role of the father is symbolic; it represents the possibility of the object of their desire. The phallus, as opposed to penis enlargement, it is of no one (neither male nor female, and is a combination of the two genders. Chasseguet-Smirgel, McDougall, Torok, Luquet Parat, Monique Cournet-Jeannin, and Jacqueline Schaeffer have all said, from the point of view of psycho-analysis. Chasseguet-Smirgel pointed out, in her perception, the fact that the girl knew about the existence of a vagina, almost from the beginning, though, she suggests that the "know-how" that can be ruled out, the unconscious, what is the girl, well knows, and you don't know. Some of his works, "penis envy" is defined as having a protective role. For many of the French feminist writers, and the body is the locus of the female, as well as a range of work that tries to capture it in its rhythms, In her book," Speculum " (1974), Irigaray explores the psycho-analysis as an awareness of the historical and philosophical determinants of the private discourse, and the analysis of their own unconscious fantasies. In addition, being a product of a patriarchal society, it can analyze what it owes to the mother. She constantly puts herself in the position where women don't have any personal identify. She emphasizes the girl by her mother's body. The girl, says Irigaray , has the mother, in a sense, in her skin, the wetness of its mucous membrane, in the vicinity of what is most intimate to share, it is in the mystery of her posture, pregnancy, childbirth, and sexual identity. Kristeva links of spiritual suppression, the real structure of the language, and describes the pre oedipal stage, as a play of the body's rhythms, and to pre linguistic exchange between the child and the child's mother. Kristeva refers to that which Plato, in the Timaeus, called the chora as the site of the undifferentiated bodily space the mother and the child share. Inside the Oedipus complex that is dominated by the last of the unified text, or cultural knowledge. This is the difference between the semiotic and the symbolic, in retrospect, for it is only by means of a symbolic of a person to have access to the semiotic. For For Kristeva, subjectivity is founded on a constitutive repression of the maternal, the chora, the semiotic, and the abject (liminal states, like pregnancy). Kristeva has been accused of leading women, a mother's job, but it is also seen as a way in order to have a better understanding on pre oedipal.. Interestingly enough, if you go back to Freud's concept of hysteria. The occurrence of the first psychoanalytic patient, Anna O., included mutism, paralysis, "time-missing," and gaps in memory: all expressing interruptions in the domain of a reality which is being denied. Psychoanalysis indicates that sexuality is only created through division and discontinuity, although femininity is the side that both represents, and tends to be represented as, the negative (of masculinity).

CONCLUSION

In the analysis, is a critical diagnostic project, you do not necessarily have the legislative or policy. Due to the development of a theory of motivation, and the non-rational forces that move and inspire us, and the idea that we are opaque rather than transparent, to ourselves, and not be able to fully self-knowledge or self-control, and psychoanalytic theory, it also challenges the rational, the human ego, and it shows that the ethical character of political and community may not be perfect, find the uncertainty in both the spiritual and political identity. Please do not assume that the unconscious is by a transgressive, or a conservative, but it is unreliable, sometimes it is beneficial for the rebellion or a rebellion, which was a strong and determined to defend the borders. Even though they are often in a complex environment and the psychoanalytic description of the unconscious and offer a feminist resource theory in both the political and the ontological investigation. Ontologically, the analysis shows a clear mental concept of, and the differences between men and women, and how we can live in our body and of our personality, and falsely informed the analysis, which is not reducible to either the social or the other of the categories. From a political point of view, the analysis provides a description of the forces, that will organize, disorganize, and the order of the relationship that the two of us. By providing insight into the formation of subjectivity, and animating fantasies, make use of the social life, the normal use, so it will also be the failure of the analysis of the enduring elements of a patriarchal social relations, including symbolic links, and the internal forces are used to support the identity, and the terminals of the sexual participants are in a relationship of domination and submission. Psychoanalytic feminism, and focus on the most important component of the society, the core of the differences between men and women in the community, helping to explain the final stage of male power, and enables feminist theorists to articulate possible correctives, problems, and ways to improve it, or ethical violations that are returned to politics and beyond, and not only in terms of the work to the public sphere.

REFERENCES

- Benjamin, Jessica. (1988). Bond's Of Love, United Kingdom: AwesomeBooks
- Chodorow, Nancy. (1978). The Reproduction of Mothering: Psychoanalysis and the Sociology of Gender, University of California Press.
- De Beauvoir, S. (1949). The Second Sex, Harmondsworth: Penguin Books Ltd.

- Firestone, Shulamith. (1970). The Dialectic of Sex: The Case for Feminist Revolution. New York: William Morrow and Company.
- Friedan, B. (1963). Feminine Mystique, Harmondsworth: Penguin Books Ltd.
- Freud, Sigmund. (1905). Three Essays on the Theory of Sexuality, London: Imago Publishing
- Greer, Germaine. (1970). The Female Eunuch, United Kingdom: MacGibbon & Kee
- Haslanger, S. (1995). "Ontology and Social Construction", Philosophical Topics, 23: 95–125.
- Hooks, Bell. (2000). Feminist Theory: From Margins to Center, London: Pluto Press.
- Jaggar, Alison. (1983) "Human Biology in Feminist Theory: Sexual Equality Reconsidered", in Beyond Domination: New Perspectives on Women and Philosophy, C. Gould (ed.), Lanham: Rowman & Littlefield Publishers, Inc.
- Jung, Carl. (1928). Two Essays on Analytical Psychology (1st ed). London: Routledge.
- Millett, Kate. (1970). Sexual Politics, London: Granada Publishing Ltd.
- Mitchell, Juliet. (1972). Psychoanalysis and feminism. UK: Penguin Books.
- Raphael-Leff, Joan, and Perelberg, Rosine Jozef (Eds.) (1997). Female experience: Three generations of British women psychoanalysts on work with women. London: Routledge.
- Renzetti, C. and D. Curran (1992). "Sex-Role Socialization", in Feminist Philosophies, J. Kourany, J. Sterba, and R. Tong (eds.), New Jersey: Prentice Hall.
- Rogers, L. (1999). Sexing the Brain, London: Phoenix.
- Wright, Elizabeth. (1992). Feminism and psychoanalysis: A critical dictionary. Oxford, UK: Blackwell.
- H. G. Baynes and C. F. Baynes. 1928. Contributions to Analytical Psychology, London: Routledge.

CHAPTER XIV

THE CONCEPT OF INTELLIGENCE: USEFUL OR USELESS?

Dr. Ekata Gupta,Associate Professor,Guru Nanak Institute of management, Delhi.
Kanishka Tomar, Pupil Teacher, Manvi Institute of Education and Technology, SCERT,Delhi.

• • •

INTRODUCTION

There is no history in the field of intelligence, but several histories depending on who says the narrative. Carroll, Herrenstein, Murray and Jensen, for example, have recounted the laudative storey somewhat differently from the most questionable tales of Gardner, Gould, Lemann, Sacks or Stanovich. Perhaps more balanced stories are Mackintosh's. Of course, there are differences in these categories of authors. These variations must be noted as while the ideological lenses are used in many fields of psychology, few areas seem to have lens colors, and some could claim that there are a lot of various flaws, such as lenses, in which understanding is observed. The different perspectives derive from the ideological preconceptions which not only influence statements but also the inclusive. For instance, Carroll versus Gardner nearly overlaps historic data used to support their conflicting intelligence ideas. In this chapter I investigate three methods to clarification of values, but there can be no genuine value-free account. First, I try to convey the views of researchers and their eras throughout the history of the subject. . Secondly, I analyse this work by pinpointing evolutional aspects and revealing what my own ideas are. Thirdly, I am dialectically seeking to represent many points of view which emphasize both the positive and the negative side of various contributions. It is understood that in the future all points of view taken in the past might be regarded as being warped by "20/20 retrospectives."

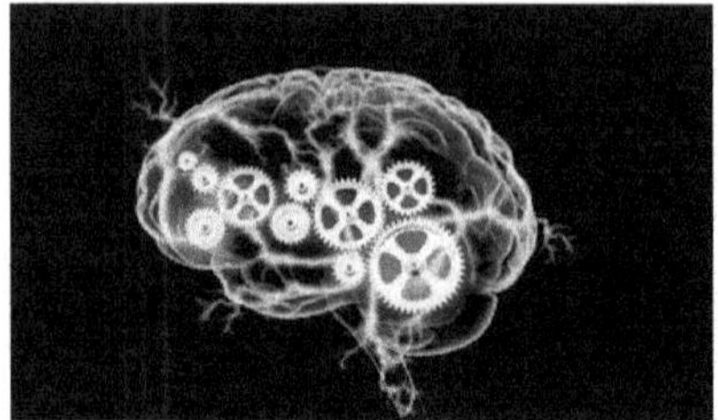

Source: https://lh3.googleusercontent.com/

A dialectic examination will be used for the full chapter. The basic premise is that good or bad core ideas are eventually a springboard for new ideas, which have developed from the previously inconsistent relations between prior ideas. This chapter focuses on the history of intelligence, in particular intelligence theories. Contemporary thinking is referenced elsewhere, as is research interesting readers. These hypotheses and research are only discussed in passing in this chapter.

Intelligence suggestions that are better understood by examining non-inclusive (i.e. novel) issues, which need Ss to utilize other concepts or form techniques. The limited successful intelligence techniques in cognitive and cognitive components are thought to be partially due to the use of more (known) tasks than they are best suited for intelligence study.

After reviewing Harlow's work on the "learning sets," the author examined the historical and empirical bases for the notion of "fixed information" and "pre-defined development" and obtained insight into Hebb's core processes, the actions of computers and programmers. In the framework of the continuing commitment with his environment, Piaget's studies on sensory motors and successive stages are examined and evaluated.

The child develops logical procedures. The authors then assess parts of Piaget's work on psychological theories in light of new ideas and facts, and try certain Piaget's notions to prove established intelligence and predictable growth.

CONCEPT OF INTELLIGENCE

The theory of ideas of Rosch, applied by the idea of intelligence, points to the fact that one's intelligence resembles one prototypically intelligent individual. Since no characteristic feature is the prototype, a process-based intelligence definition cannot be stated appropriately. As a rule, combining numerous experimental measurements into a single index, such in a Binet test, would be appropriate. In fact, it is just difficult to measure many of the important traits. His paper provides a definition of intelligence that includes the mental ability to adapt to, and to pick and shape, any environment. Although the conduct described as intelligent may change from one environmental situation to another, the mental processes behind this activity are not. According to this definition. However, the capacity of an individual to use these procedures may vary from one setting to another. The capacity is used to achieve exterior world correspondence and internal coherence between diverse systems of knowledge and belief. There is a discussion on the usefulness of the concept to comprehend contemporary theories, intelligence tests, and the function of intelligence in lifelong learning.

This editorial discusses current developments in intelligence, especially with regard to response times and the average evocative potential based on experimental evidence. First, it was claimed that the notion of a general intelligence factor should not be abandoned, as many contemporary researchers have shown. It is not just valuable but also necessary in terms of explaining empirical evidence provided through confirmation factor analyses, multidimensional scale, and so on. In addition, attempts to explain the difference between the learning, cultural and environmental and educational variables in cognitive operation cannot be held accountable for recent evidence that exhibits high correlations between basic physiological (evocated) potential (effect times, movement times, inspection times) and perceptual motor processes (IQ). The controversy about the meaning of intelligence was largely caused by the incapacity to meet threefold intelligence criteria and the fact that summarized experimental evidence and theoretical issues should be considered in any acceptable theory. These have produced a "fresh appearance" in the notion of intelligence (Eysenck, 1986).

TYPES OF INTELLIGENCE

The ideas of implicit intelligence were investigated with exemplary intelligence surveys. Examination 1 was a four-sample study of remarkable cases. These different samples showed similar numbers of popular specimens split into five groups. There were five forms of intelligence: science, art, business, communication and moral intelligence. Study 2 has rejected the idea that, because of the little overlap between intelligence and the tales of famousness, inventiveness and wisdom, the example stories are both indiscriminate and available. In Study 3, 50 famous persons were evaluated as compared with individual intellectual specimens. The popularity of each five ratings was outstanding. 31 percent were not known for outstanding Study 4 reports include not just famous people (friends, family members, teachers, etc.). The data demonstrate that five implied types of intellect play a role in people's ideas, each highly available.

Scientific Intelligence

During World War II, scientist intelligence was coined, but despite its antiquity and relative importance it has not received the respect it should have had. The interest in the WMD programmes is unexpectedly growing recently. The key components of scientific intelligence are presented in This essay, aiming to investigate the definition and functioning of scientific intelligence and its significant problems. This seeks to establish an agenda in this crucial subject for future study.

Artistic Intelligence

In the financial, medicinal and educational industries, machinery learning (ML) is used to develop smart stock forecasts, health robots and virtual support, for instance. However, its usage has mainly not been used by the artistic expression in one of the most human endeavors. Present ML applications in creative projects use primarily artificial agents in order to enhance human capability to regions where huge data have access to untapped human artists' connections. These examples initially look at human beings and only enhance human ability to build new musical combinations based on a basic range of tones, to analyse photographic material to pick styles for future image modifications or to combine poetic language based on phonetic similarities, for example. While ML is employed in such applications as a data mining agent for unknown domains, it does not exceed the predicted human constraints. In everything with which we engage, we use Artificial intelligence (AI) in unexpected ways, another field in which the ML enables artistic expression. Imagine talking, for example, to a guy who responds with Google Assistant or to a robotic person who wants to use drugs secretly. I recommend using ML to generate new behavior such that unknown preset training settings for users can modify these behaviors. The application of ML to unexpected types of interaction alters what computers we think are able to do. They provide occasions in which the meaning of intelligence for mankind transcends beyond human assumptions.

ENTREPRENURIAL INTELLIGENCE

The entrepreneur has identified entrepreneurial research as a catalyst for the new entrepreneurial process. The study of the emotional intelligence of business executives was a popular line of research that has not yet been applied to entrepreneurship. This web-based study collected emotional skills data on successful young entrepreneurs. Participating entrepreneurs indicated high standards of self-assurance, confidence, performance direction, service orientation, a catalyst for change, cooperation and collaboration. Confidence, the capacity to retain norms of integrity and honesty, rated best among 18 tested emotional skills. The findings also stress the significance of teamwork and partnership in the new venture process.

Communicative Intelligence

In the unexpectedly dynamic field of human interaction CI is the purposeful and intentional use of verbal and nonverbal models of communication so as to create links across cultures and civilizations (see Zoller, 2008). Moreover, the author believes that CI is a deliberately conscious condition where verbal and nonverbal abilities and motions are utilized to match the message with the way in which relationships, model empathy and trust in impact are viewed. By adopting CI's techniques and approaches, leaders may improve the quality of their relations, leading to new opportunities and solutions to the problems that companies face. Key themes of interest, including how CI may influence intercultural collaboration and leadership, will be explored.

Moral Intelligence

Moral intelligence is newer and less researched, but it has a tremendous potential to increase our knowledge of learning and behaviour than existing cognitive, emotional and social intelligentsia. The capacity to apply ethical concepts to individual objectives, beliefs and behaviours is moral understanding. The structure of moral intelligence consists of four competences, three competences, forgiveness and compassion. Morally intelligent school leaders and instructors will encourage, respect and care for their kids and provide rise to them. This article explores what morals are and how leaders, teachers and children may be taught. It will be discussing its link with character and ethical conduct, and the other intelligences. The development of increased moral intelligence will lead to more constructive organizations, better connections and pupils who are both intelligent and decent, and who appreciate universal human rights and ideals.

THEORIES OF INTELLIGENCE

Guilford's Structure of Intellect

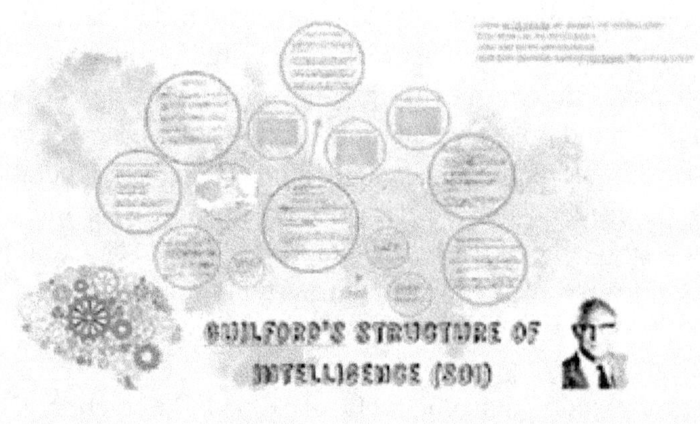

Source: https://encrypted-tbn0.gstatic.com/

J. P. Guilford was extremely influential in creative psychology. He is the father of contemporary creative research in many respects. Yet in certain aspects, we propose, his idea of creativity was faulty. In this essay we explore both Guilford's approach to creativity's benefits and limits. Theory shows that Procrustean methods of factoring may be utilized to deliver results which appear to support randomly defined hypotheses. This can be achieved even though:

(a) variables have been confidential and probably inter-related legally;

(b) orthogonal loading of factors;

(c) interpretation factor loadings have to be at least .30; and

(d) S samples are as large as 175, 205 and 240.

Results are understood to indicate a lack of convincing factor-analytic support to the SI theory since this is not significantly better than support for random-generated theories.

In the framework of capitalization on chance, the structure-of-intellect (SI) Theory is assessed. In the study of human intelligence, this empiric difficulty is brought within a broader view of the general conceptual usefulness of theory. There were numerous remarkable aspects of the analytical factor support for theory. At most, studies to support the concept should be seen as experimental. However, the model provided an effective strategy for testing and for showing intriguing ideas regarding intellectual characteristics. However, there are several difficulties with theory even in this situation. The idea simply gives a static taxonomy and hence provides extremely little opportunity to analyse developmental problems.

Howard Gardener's Theory

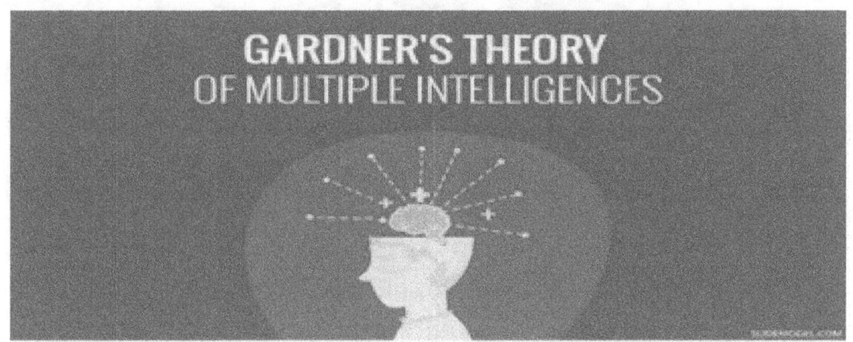

Source: https://cdn2.slidemodel.com/

New and more contextualized cognitive tasks are proposed as alternatives to more standard psychometric tests in the multiple intelligence paradigm. The aim of this essay is to explore whether or not these two sorts of devices converge into a generic cognitive component. A set of Gardner's multiple intellectual appraisal tasks, (language, logical, visual/spatial, body kinesthetic, naturalistic and musical intelligence), were administered to 294 children aged 5 to 7, including the battery of general and differential aptitudes (BADyG: reasoning, memory, oral aptitude, numerical aptitude and spatial aptitude). The confirmatory factor analysis shows that both batteries are without a single general factor, showing instead the presence of two general factors that collect the tests they include. Moreover, these 2 general variables are consistent with traditional and multiple intelligence evaluations and demonstrate a statistically modest connection. These results contradict the initial stance of Gardner to refuse a generic intelligence component, especially in the context of measurements that do not correspond to more typical intelligence tests.

Source: https://cdn.slidesharecdn.com/

Gardner says it contains seven different intellectual units in the human organism. He identifies these units with their respective intelligences which are seen and quantifiable. The intellect hypothesis of Gardner is investigated in the framework of g, whereas the work of cognitive style theoreticians compares Gardner's Ml theory. This research indicates that Ml theory did not find new "intelligences," but revised what other people classified as cognitive styles.

Goleman's Emotional Intelligence

The principles from Daniel Goleman's book are brought to work using Emotional Intelligence. Corporate leaders and leading performers are identified not by their IQs or their talents, but via their "emotional intelligence." These are a series of abilities that differentiate how individuals are managing, interacting and communicating their feelings. Dozens of specialists in 500 companies, government agencies and NGOs throughout the world have analyzed the barometer of excellence in almost all jobs. This book discusses what is emotional intelligence and why it matters for excellence in the work more than IQ or knowledge. It contains 12 individual skills (e.g., correct self-evaluation, self-control, initiative and optimism) and 13 essential relational skills (such as service orientation, developing others, conflict management, and building bonds). Goleman contains several instances and storey from Fortune 500 to non-profit pre-school, showing how these skills are leading to or countering success.

Emotional intelligence includes a range of qualities including self-control, enthusiasm and tenacity. The key elements of anger, conflict management, empathy development, and impulses must be taught to every kid. Schools must support youngsters in their emotions recognition and management. In caring, respectful relationships with kids, educators should demonstrate emotional intelligence.

CONCLUSION

Research with delayed children and adults is one way of studying intelligence. Any definition of how they vary from non-retarded persons leads to a specification of essential intelligence components. We discuss two main topics of inquiry in this paper. One is that study with the retarded has managed to discover a key element of intelligence, centered on the role of control processes in memory and problem solving circumstances. The results of numerous experiments led us to the conclusion that intelligence is a hallmark for generalizing information from one state to the next and this ability depends on efficient "executive monitoring." We suggest that comparative/developmental work is necessary to gain a better knowledge in areas where fewer late-film research has been done. We demonstrate this by debating some work aimed at identifying individual parameter variations reflecting fundamental components of generic information processing systems.

To anticipate our ultimate conclusion, we support an intelligence perspective based on the executive of the invention and implementation of planning activities which can light the evolution of general theory in a major portion of intelligence.

REFRENCES

- Oddson, R. J. (2013). Intelligence. Wiley & Sons Inc. John Inc.
- J. M. Hunt. Hunt (1961). Smartness and expertise.
- Oddson, R. J. (1981). Smartness and no tranquilization. Psychological Education Journal, 73(1), 1.
- Nietz, U. (1979). The intelligence idea. Smart, 3(3), 217-227.
- Oddson, R. J. (1997). The intelligence notion and its significance in lifelong learning and achievement. Psychologist from the United States, 10(52), 1030.
- Odds, M. J. J. (1988). "Intelligence" concept: useful or ineffective? Smart, 12(1), 1-16.

- L., Wehr, P., Harms, P. D., & Richmond, D. I. (2002). Exemplary surveys have been used to disclose implicit intelligence kinds. Bulletin on Humanity and Social Psychology, 28(8), 1051-1062.
- Goodman. - Goodman, M. S. (2009). The paradigm of Jones: how, why, and why scientific intelligence. National Security Intelligence, 24(2), 236-256.
- Michael, M. (2020). Critikos. Artistic Intelligence.
- S. & White, R. J. Rhee, K. S. (2007). Entrepreneurs' emotional intelligence. Little Entrepreneurship Journal, 20(4), 409-425.
- Customs, C. C. (2015). The ideology promoting cross-cultural collaboration by employing communication intelligence. Intercultural partnership and leadership in modern enterprises (pp. 303-320). Overall IGI.
- Sky, R. H. R. (2009). Moral school-based intelligence. Entry online.
- Müll, A., & Krausch, M. L. J. (2001). Intellectual model and creative model structure of Guilford: Contributions and constraints. Review of Creativity, 13(3-4), 309-316.
- Knapp, J. L., & Horn, J. L. (1973). About the subjective nature of the empirical foundation of Guilford's intellectual framework.
- Hans, J. O. & Klaus, J. L. J. (1977). Guilford's critical assessment of intellect-structure theory. Smart, 1(1), 65-81.
- Almeida, L. S., M. D., Klaus, M. A., R. M., Holm, R., M. & Krebz, J. M. (2010). Assessment of intelligence: the Gardner hypothesis of multiple intelligence. Individual differences in learning and learning, 20(3), 225-230.
- Morgan, H. - Morgan, H. (1996). Gardner's multiple intelligence theory is analysed. Review, 263-269, 18(4).
- Goleman, D. Goleman, D. (1998). Emotional intelligence working.
- O'Neil, J. Alice (1996). Emotional Intelligence: a talk to Daniel Goleman. Leadership of education, 54(1), 6-11. Education.
- J. C., & Brown, A. L. S. (1978). Intelligence theory: contributions from delayed children's study. Caution, 2(3), 279-304.

CHAPTER XV

UNDERSTANDING AND MANAGING DISRUPTIVE BEHAVIOR IN ADOLESCENTS

Dr.Mukta Goyal, Principal,Manvi Institute of Education & Technololgy, SCERT, Delhi.

• • •

INTRODUCTION

Adolescence is frequently associated with behavioural issues. Student disruption, aggression, and academic failure are widespread issues in schools across the country. Adolescence is a time when people learn to be self-sufficient. Adolescents typically assert their independence by questioning or challenging, and sometimes breaking, rules. Parents and doctors must distinguish between isolated instances of poor judgment and a pattern of misbehaviour that necessitates professional intervention. The severity and frequency of infractions serve as indicators. Regular drinking, frequent episodes of fighting, absenteeism without permission (truancy), and theft, for example, are far more serious than isolated episodes of the same activities. Other warning signs include poor academic performance and running away from home. Adolescents who cause serious injury or use a weapon in a fight are of particular concern.

Adolescents are often out of the direct physical control of adults because they are much more independent and mobile than children were. Adolescents' behaviour is governed by their own moral and behavioural code in these circumstances. Parents' guide rather than directly control their children's behaviour. Adolescents who feel loved and supported by their parents are less likely to engage in risky behaviour. Adolescents whose parents communicate clear expectations about their children's behaviour are also more likely to succeed.

Authoritarian parenting is a parenting style in which children help to set family expectations and rules. This parenting style is more likely to promote mature behaviours than authoritarian parenting (in which parents make decisions with little input from their children) or permissive parenting (in which parents set few limits).

Authoritarian parenting employs a system of graduated privileges in which adolescents are first given small amounts of responsibility (such as caring for a pet, doing household chores, purchasing clothing, decorating their room, or managing an allowance). When adolescents handle a responsibility or privilege well over time, more responsibilities and privileges are granted, such as going out with friends without parents and driving. Poor judgment or a lack of responsibility, on the other hand, results in the loss of privileges. Each new privilege necessitates close parental supervision to ensure that adolescents follow the agreed-upon rules.

Disruptive behaviour, which is more common in males, is clinically significant behaviour that disrupts the adolescent's interpersonal context. Adolescents who exhibit disruptive behaviour lack the ability to self-regulate affect and behaviour, which is required for social adaptation. This self-regulation deficit is shaped by biological vulnerability (e.g. Temperament, genetics), as well as the regulating and developmental influence of family function.

Adolescence is the time when a person transitions from childhood to adulthood. It involves significant physical and psychological changes in a young person's life. ... Understanding what to expect at different stages of adolescence and early adulthood might help to encourage healthy development.

Externalizing Adolescent Problem Behaviors

Externalizing Adolescent Problem Behaviors such as Delinquent behavior, Aggression, and Adult Crime Later Adolescence has been viewed as a developmental stage in the individual's life. Across studies conducted in the 1990s, there has been an increase in the prevalence of both internalizing and externalizing disorders among youth. Externalizing problem behaviors are generally demonstrated to be a robust finding (Keil& Price, 2006).

Moffitt (1993) defines formalized among cross-sectional studies, two general types of adolescent problem behavior as clinically relevant externalizing behavior problems, i.e. overtly aggressive behavior, are described along the two dimensions.

Dimensions such as inhibition versus aggression (Miller, 1967), over controlled versus empirically based multivariate studies (Frick, Lahey, Loeber; under controlled (Achenbach & Edelbrock, 1978), or internalizing Tannenbaum, Van Horn, Christ, 1993 have been identified. Relationships with internalizing versus externalizing issues (Achenbach, 1966; 1991). It has also been discovered that antisocial peers are related to the

Aggression and juvenile delinquency are typical examples of externalizing behavior emergence (Elliott, Huizinger, &Ageton, externalizing problem behavior. Internalizing behavioral issues (1985), particularly when these relationships are strained.

Adolescence is recognised by the World Health Organization (WHO) and the United Nations as the period between the ages of 10 and 19.

Adolescence is a period of growth and development. The existence or absence of a number of intervening and moderating influences and contextual elements will invariably determine whether adolescents' life meaning and wisdom will grow and unfold from being relatively straightforward to being mature and complex. The complete absence of these moderating forces may stifle the development of personal meaning, but their partial presence may promote and even expedite the search for personal meaning in life among teenagers. Both personal meaning and wisdom are seen to have their origins in interpersonal relationships and social transactions during adolescence, requiring teenagers to engage in discussion and discourse with peers and other reference groups. According to studies, 30% of adolescents wish to work in a field that allows them to make a positive difference in the world. Adolescents who had purposeful job goals also reported higher meaning in their lives and schooling, according to regression analysis. Adolescence, on the other hand, is often connected with puberty and the cycle of physical changes that leads to reproductive maturity in many countries. In other cultures, adolescence is defined in broader terms that include psychological, social, and moral components of maturation as well as the strictly physical aspects. Adolescence is marked by an increase in abstract thinking, knowledge, and logical reasoning skills.

This is when the majority of behavioural issues arise. The types of problems vary depending on the child's age and might encompass a wide range of issues. Adolescents are particularly vulnerable to mental illnesses.

Adolescence is characterised by a great deal of emotional and behavioural upheaval. While adhering to conventional rules, the adolescent fights to create his uniqueness. They have been exposed to societal changes as a result of rapid urbanisation and modernisation. The teenager is more vulnerable to dysfunctional thinking and behaviour as a result of the collapse in family structure and excessive or insufficient control. The proper resolution of these emotional and behavioural issues is necessary for adulthood to be healthy. Most adolescents successfully navigate this tightrope and reach adulthood. Not every adolescent will be lucky enough to receive the necessary societal support for a successful transition. Some people acquire maladaptive emotional and behavioural tendencies. This portends a bleak future for the individual, leading in sadness, delinquency, and suicide, among other issues. Adolescents are experiencing an increase in the prevalence of mental illness and maladaptive behaviours. According to WHO estimates, up to 20% of adolescents have one or more mental or behavioural issues. Adolescents with behavioural and emotional difficulties are shown to be prevalent in 16.5 percent to 40.8 percent of the time, according to studies conducted around the world. 6 and in India, it ranges from 13.7 percent to 50 percent. Adolescents account for one-fifth of India's population, implying a significant disease burden on the country. According to a literature analysis, the prevalence rate of emotional and behavioural issues among teenagers in India ranges from 13.7% to 50%. According to research, 75% of adolescents who thought they were performing poorly academically actually had behavioural/emotional issues. 43 percent of teenagers who believed their parents were dissatisfied with their academic performance developed the mental health problem mentioned above. Adolescents' emotional and behavioural problems were found to be linked to parental disagreement. Inter-parental conflict has been found to be a significant predictor of adolescent suicide. Family ties are an essential protective factor in war-affected adolescents that needs to be investigated further by gender.

Adolescence is a time when people learn to be self-sufficient.

Adolescents usually demonstrate their independence by questioning or challenging rules, and perhaps breaking them. Parents and doctors must be able to tell the difference between an occasional lapse in judgement and a pattern of misbehaviour that necessitates professional intervention. Infractions' severity and frequency serve as indicators. Regular drinking, frequent fights, truancy (absenteeism without permission), and stealing, for example, are all significantly more serious than isolated incidents of the same behaviour. Other warning indicators include a drop in academic performance and a desire to flee the house. Adolescents who cause serious injury or use a weapon in a fight are of particular concern.

Adolescents are often out of the direct physical control of parents because they are considerably more autonomous and mobile than youngsters.

Adolescents' behaviour is dictated by their own moral and behavioural code in these situations. Parents should guide rather than direct their children's actions. Parents who provide warmth and support to their children are less likely to engage in dangerous behaviour. Adolescents who have clear expectations for their behaviour and who have constant limit setting and monitoring from their parents are less likely to participate in dangerous behaviours. An alarming proportion of our teenagers suffer from emotional and behavioural issues that have their origins in the home.

Then there are sleep issues, which are widespread in adolescence and have a severe impact on adolescents' mental health and functioning. Biological rhythms varies from person to person. Some people are morning people, preferring intellectual and physical activity in the morning, while others are evening people. There were links between this morningness-eveningness construct and several elements of mental health and well-being; for example, eveningness was linked to depression and seasonal affective disorders.

Adolescents who have more evenings have more challenges.

Eveningness and sleeplessness are both frequent in adolescents, but it's unclear if they have a separate or combined effect on the likelihood of psychopathology. Evening-type teenagers were more likely to experience insomnia symptoms. Evenings and insomnia were found to be independently linked to an increased risk of emotional and behavioural issues. Eveningness and sleeplessness symptoms are both risk factors for adolescent mental illness. When analysing and treating psychopathology in adolescents, it's important to include both sleep and circadian aspects. Boys were twice as likely as girls to break the rules or engage in delinquent behaviour. Adolescents have become increasingly accustomed to consuming energy drinks. Boys and older teens were more likely to consume energy drinks on a regular basis. Adolescents from middle-income families were less likely to consume energy drinks on a regular basis. Adolescents who used energy drinks on a daily basis had greater health and behavioural issues, as well as less positive school experiences. When researchers looked at the relationship between various socio-environmental factors and emotional and behavioural problems in adolescents, they discovered that children whose parents were addicted to alcohol or illicit drugs had up to three times as many behavioural and emotional problems as children whose parents were not addicted.

Alcoholism was discovered to be the most common addiction,

with adolescents from addicted households having a threefold higher frequency of behavioural and emotional difficulties. Young people whose parents were alcoholics were more likely to seek help from friends and siblings than from their parents. Cigarette smoking was found to be highly linked to greater levels of emotional and behavioural issues. The emotional/behavioral health of adolescents may be useful in the creation of effective anti-smoking programmes in the classroom and elsewhere. Globally, chronic diseases and disorders are on the rise. An ageing population and socioeconomic changes are contributing to a continuous rise in these prevalent and expensive long-term health issues. Adolescents with chronic illnesses have also been found to be significantly linked to problems. Asthma and other chronic respiratory tract diseases, musculoskeletal issues, and heart disease are the most frequent of these conditions. Adolescents are more prone than healthy controls to acquire mental and behavioural disorders, have a greater incidence of at least one psychiatric diagnosis, and are depressed or have low self-esteem.

Adolescents with a history of physical abuse were nearly twice as likely to have behavioural and emotional issues.

Abused children had a seven-fold increased risk of developing a serious depressive condition. Abused boys were shown to have the same risk of getting depression as abused girls. The mechanism by which an increase in life stress can lead to emotional and behavioural disorders in adolescents is through negative automatic thinking. Adolescents from refugee and migrant families may be at a higher risk of developing emotional and behavioural issues. Migrant teenagers have had more traumatic experiences and have more peer issues and avoidance behaviours. Non-migrant teenagers, on the other hand, show higher anxiety, externalising difficulties, and hyperactivity. The frequency of traumatic experiences experienced, gender, and living condition are all factors that influence the prevalence of emotional and behavioural issues. Although the prevalence of emotional and behavioural symptoms in migrant and non-migrant adolescents is similar, special attention should be paid to the screening and support of vulnerable groups within the migrant population, such as girls, those who have experienced numerous traumatic events, and unaccompanied refugee children and adolescents. Adolescents with behavioural issues had a more negative assessment of the environment when it came to most of the variables linked to family, school, and peers. Clearly, behavioural issues are linked to issues in a variety of settings. Multiple regression analyses revealed that problems at school were the most important predictor of behavioural problem scores for boys, whereas problems at home were the most important predictor of behavioural problem scores for girls. Furthermore, living in a disadvantaged neighbourhood is linked to more behavioural issues, which may worsen as children transition from childhood to adolescent. The neighbourhood environment must be included in public health programmes to improve child mental health. Furthermore, consistent genetic affects were detected throughout ages, demonstrating that genetic factors exhibited as early as age 4 years support biological basis underlying adolescent behavioural disorders. At each age, however, genetic and environmental changes were detected. This suggests that while genetic variables are crucial for understanding stable individual differences in behavioural disorders across childhood and adolescence, fresh genetic effects can also help transform such behaviours. Higher levels of physical activity and a higher parental socioeconomic status were linked to better overall academic achievement and future goals for higher education in fully adjusted models. High behavioural problem scores were associated with inferior overall academic achievement and future academic intentions. In conclusion, higher levels of physical activity, less behavioural difficulties, and a higher socioeconomic status were all linked to high self-perceived overall academic performance and plans for higher education among adolescents. The interrelationships of these elements, as well as the beneficial link between physical activity, mental health, and school results, provide a vital backdrop for future research, intervention programming, and policy aimed at enhancing adolescent educational attainment. While emotional and behavioural issues put youth's development at risk, resilience allows them to adapt and overcome adversity.

DISRUPTIVE BEHAVIOUR COMPONENTS

Disruptive behaviour is a component of many disorders, but a disease model does not fully explain it. Descriptive diagnostic statements provide clinicians with information about what youth do. They do not, however, explain why the behaviour occurs, nor do they outline treatments to manage the behaviour. In order to do so, one must look to the emerging field of developmental psychopathology and the impact of family function on self-regulation.

Some of the most problematic externalizing behaviours are lying, stealing, vandalism, truancy, arson, promiscuity, defiance toward authority, disinhibit ion (severe impulsivity), and aggression (threatening, bullying, fighting, rape).Reasons for seeing a child and adolescent psychiatrist Outside of the family, such as schoolmates and teachers, the disruptive behaviour may pose a problem.

The psychiatric evaluation of children with disruptive behaviour follows the standard evaluation format, with special areas of investigation for the disruptive adolescent (Table 1). The first step in making a treatment decision is to collect detailed psychiatric and medical histories from both the adolescent and his or her family. A neuropsychological/psychological evaluation, brain imaging (MRI, CT), or electroencephalography are examples of additional assessments.

Those who have been impacted by the adolescent's disruptive behaviour (Parents, classmates, and extended family) provide critical information such as age of onset, type of behaviour (e.g., aggressive), and precipitating factors. As a result, the clinician can evaluate the interactional component: Who is impacted? Where does the disruption happen? When does it usually happen?

It is critical to observe the interaction between the parent(s) and the adolescent. A parent's harshness, inconsistency, or indulgence can have a significant impact on their child's behaviour. A mental status examination that assesses intellectual ability and communication skills, aggressive/ homicidal ideation, paranoia or other psychotic symptoms, and empathy capacity should also be included in the evaluation. Treatment sequencing for adolescent disruptive behaviour.

In the treatment of disruptive youth, interventions should be integrated or sequenced.

This proposed sequence includes some early family and parent work to disrupt individual symptom-maintaining family interactions, without which individual work fails:

• Use pharmacology and parent management training to stabilize behaviour.

• Use family therapy to assist with the interactive process.

• Recognize individual family dynamics that necessitate intervention.

• As the adolescent grows older, encourage individual adolescent therapy (e.g., cognitive-behavioural, interpersonal, psychodynamic, or supportive).

• Take into account larger systemic issues.

Residential treatment and multisystem treatment are examples of interventions.

The treatment of medical illness, which addresses substance abuse when present and uses psychopharmacology to treat severe symptoms, stabilizes acute behaviour. It is illegal to prescribe medication for nonspecific, developmentally mediated disruptiveness. However, it is not illegal to prescribe medications for specific disorders (e.g., ADHD, bipolar disorder, autism), which can include disruptive behaviour as part of the core condition.

These biological interventions should be accompanied by parent management training with an adolescent focus. This type of training provides immediate strategies for behaviour control through the use of behavioural cues. Second, an assessment of the family, informed by various schools and techniques of family therapy, frequently dictates the need for intervention. Unfortunately, due to specific parental and marital dynamics, parent management interventions are frequently not implemented.

CONCLUSION:

A sizable portion of our adolescent population requires assistance in dealing with emotional and behavioural issues. Though many children from troubled families may appear normal, understanding the family context and the challenges that teenagers face helps to identify the adolescent-family dyad that requires treatment. It points to the necessity for a multifaceted approach to preventing these issues in teenagers. School-based mental health programmes can effectively address the problem by assisting victims as soon as possible. A community intervention for addiction may be necessary, and schools can serve as the focal point by implementing innovative initiatives such as student drama clubs, street plays, and other activities that educate both the family and the schoolchildren about the dangers of addiction. Although there is mounting evidence that energy drink intake is linked to detrimental social, emotional, and health effects, few studies have looked at this link in teenagers. Adolescents who consume energy drinks are at risk for a variety of harmful consequences and should be targeted for prevention. As a result, we might deduce that a loving family with marital harmony is protective against mental illness. As a parent, the most important thing you can do is accept and help your children as they are. Explain to your adolescent why they shouldn't experiment with drugs, alcohol, or sex so early in their lives. Rather than dismissing their feelings, attempt to listen and empathise with them. Encourage them to come to you if they have a problem rather than keeping it to themselves. Instead of being confrontational or violent, teach kids appropriate ways to vent frustration.

Teenagers are perplexed and want direction in order to stay on the right track. They require boundaries in order to maintain control. When you make rules, you're also setting restrictions for people to follow. Teenage years are an excellent time to begin teaching decision-making abilities. Teach students how to analyse or gauge an option in a variety of ways so they can make the best decision possible.

Cognitive-behavioural therapy and skill training may be beneficial, particularly if there is comorbidity (eg, depression). While psychodynamic psychotherapy provides a framework for understanding developmental constructs, it has not been proven to be effective as a stand-alone treatment intervention. Finally, behaviourally oriented parent management training programs are perhaps the most empirically validated modality.

Working with disruptive adolescents has the ultimate goal of improving self-regulation in all domains. Although difficult, this is the foundation of child and adolescent development. Such development occurs within the family, and any treatment must support the efforts of the family who is raising children to instil the basic life skill of self-control.

REFERENCES

- Fry, P. S. (1998). The development of personal meaning and wisdom in adolescence: A reexamination of moderating and consolidating factors and influences. Lawrence Erlbaum Associates Publishers.
- Yeager, D. S., & Bundick, M. J. (2009). The role of purposeful work goals in promoting meaning in life and in schoolwork during adolescence. Journal of Adolescent Research, 24(4), 423-452.
- Pathak, R., Sharma, R. C., Parvan, U. C., Gupta, B. P., Ojha, R. K., & Goel, N. K. (2011). Behavioural and emotional problems in school going adolescents. The Australasian medical journal, 4(1), 15.
- Holubcikova, J., Kolarcik, P., Geckova, A. M., Reijneveld, S. A., & van Dijk, J. P. (2017). Regular energy drink consumption is associated with the risk of health and behavioural problems in adolescents. European journal of pediatrics, 176(5), 599-605.
- Lange, L., & Randler, C. (2011). Morningness-eveningness and behavioural problems in adolescents. Sleep and Biological Rhythms, 9(1), 12-18.
- Flouri, E., & Panourgia, C. (2014). Negative automatic thoughts and emotional and behavioural problems in adolescence. Child and Adolescent Mental Health, 19(1), 46-51.

- Derluyn, I., Broekaert, E., & Schuyten, G. (2008). Emotional and behavioural problems in migrant adolescents in Belgium. European child & adolescent psychiatry, 17(1), 54-62.
- Kantomaa, M. T., Tammelin, T. H., Demakakos, P., Ebeling, H. E., & Taanila, A. M. (2010). Physical activity, emotional and behavioural problems, maternal education and self-reported educational performance of adolescents. Health education research, 25(2), 368-379.
- Hasan, A., & Husain, A. (2016). Behavioural problems of adolescents. IAHRW International Journal of Social Sciences, 4(2), 238-244.
- https://www.psychiatrictimes.com/view/synthetic-cannabinoids-cathinones
- https://www.psychiatrictimes.com/view/understanding-and-managing-adolescent-disruptive-behavior

CHAPTER XVI

COGNITIVE AND MORAL DEVELOPMENT IN LEARNERS

Mr. K. C. Malik, Retired Associate Professor, Sri Venkateswara College, University of Delhi.

• • •

INTRODUCTION

COGNITIVE DEVELOPMENT

Cognitive development means how children think, explore and figure things out. It is the growth of information, skills, problem-solving abilities, and attitudes that enable children to think about and comprehend the world around them. Cognitive development includes brain development. Attention, short-term memory, long-term memory, logic & reasoning, auditory processing, visual processing, and processing speed are all cognitive capabilities. They are the abilities that the brain employs to think, learn, read, remember, focus, and solve issues.

Source: www.lumenlearning.com

Children gather, sort, and analyse data from their environment, which they then use to improve their perceptual and thinking skills. Early in life, the essential character of intelligence is established, and development entails the accumulation of increasingly more learning experiences.

VIEWS OF PIAGET, BRUNER AND VYGOTSKY ON COGNITIVE DEVELOPMENT

JEAN PIAGET

Source: www.thefamouspeople.com

During the twentieth century, Jean Piaget (1896-1980) was one of the most influential researchers in the field of developmental psychology. Piaget was educated in biology and philosophy and referred to himself as a "genetic epistemologist." He was particularly interested in biological influences on "how we learn." He claimed that our ability to undertake "abstract symbolic reasoning" is what sets us apart from other animals. Piaget's ideas are frequently contrasted with those of Lev Vygotsky (1896-1934), who saw social interaction as the major wellspring of cognition and behaviour. Piaget became interested in how children think while working at Binet's IQ test facility in Paris. He saw that young children's replies were qualitatively different from older children's, implying that the younger ones were not stupid than their older friends, but rather answered the questions differently because they thought differently. The importance of Piaget's ideas on child psychology today can be summarised by his views on education and teacher training. Although Jean Piaget's theory of cognitive development is well-known, most sociologists are unfamiliar with his name. Although Piaget was primarily interested in individual development, he felt that child-to-child interaction plays a role in cognitive development. Since the last formulations of Piaget's constructivism four decades ago, cognitive developmental psychology has undergone profound alterations. Theories of cognitive development have sparked long and bitter debates that have been heavy on rhetoric but light on facts. Piagetian views of cognitive development as arising from self-directed behaviour throughout infancy are the foundations of constructivist theory. Because Piaget's views on childhood were so well-known and accepted, at least one component of development seemed certain to many psychologists: human infants went through a long time in which they are unable to reason. They can learn to recognise items and grin at them, as well as crawl and control objects, but they lack conceptions and ideas. This time, which Piaget dubbed the sensorimotor stage of development, was thought to last until a child was one-and-a-half to two years old. Infants learn how to represent the world in a symbolic, conceptual man? Ner near the end of this stage, and thus progress from infancy to early childhood. According to Jean Piaget's theory of cognitive development, children's intellect evolves through time. A kid's cognitive growth entails more than just collecting information; the youngster must also create or develop a mental picture of the world. Piaget stressed universal cognitive change as a result.

Bruner, Jerome Seymour, was an American psychologist who made significant contributions to human cognitive psychology and educational psychology's cognitive learning theory. Jerome Bruner, a psychologist by training, has always been and continues to be one of the most influential individuals in education. In the 1960s and 1970s, his educational philosophy had a direct impact on the educational programmes that were developed throughout those decades. Bruner believes that learners develop their own knowledge by employing a coding system to organise and categorise information. Bruner believed that discovering a coding system rather than being informed by a teacher is the most efficient approach to do so.

JEROME SEYMOUR BRUNER

Source: www.washingtonpost.com

Jerome Bruner was a key figure in the Cognitive Revolution, which brought behaviourism to an end in American psychology and put cognition at the forefront. Bruner argues for the primacy of 'meaning-making' in human action in his reassessment of the cognitive revolution, saying that toddlers learn to give meaning to what individuals do as they learn the language and social practices of their culture. The importance of attribution of mental states to others has been examined extensively in a new research area known as children's "theory of mind" over the last decade.

Unlike Bruner, who views psychology as a natural empirical science, researchers in this discipline consider the child as developing a causal theory to explain and predict human behaviour.

LEV SEMYONOVICH VYGOTSKY

Source: www.curriculumsolutions.com

Lev Semyonovich Vygotsky was a Soviet psychologist who specialised in child psychological development. Over the last several decades, Lev Vygotsky's (1934) work has served as the foundation for much research and theory in cognitive development, notably what has come to be known as sociocultural theory. Human development is viewed as a socially mediated process in which children acquire cultural values, beliefs, and problem-solving skills through collaborative conversations with more informed members of society, according to Vygotsky's sociocultural theory. Culture-specific tools, private speech, and the Zone of Proximal Development are all notions in Vygotsky's theory. Vygotsky's theories emphasise the importance of social contact in the formation of cognition (Vygotsky, 1978), since he strongly believed that community plays an important role in the process of "creating meaning."

Unlike Piaget, who believed that children's growth must come first, Vygotsky believed that "learning is an essential and universal part of the process of establishing culturally organised, specifically human psychological function." Vygotsky pioneered a sociocultural perspective on cognitive development. He formed his theories at roughly the same time that Jean Piaget was starting to develop his ideas (1920's and 30's), but he died at the age of 38, and so his theories remain incomplete – although some of his publications are currently being translated from Russian. Vygotsky emphasises the role of culture in cognitive development. Vygotsky believes that cognitive development differs by culture. Vygotsky lays a greater emphasis on the social aspects that influence cognitive development. For learning, Vygotsky emphasises the importance of cultural and social context. Children and their partners co-construct knowledge as a result of social interactions from guided learning within the zone of proximal development. Vygotsky emphasises the function of language in cognitive development more (and in a different way) than others. Cognitive development, according to Vygotsky, is the product of linguistic internalisation. Adults, according to Vygotsky, are a crucial source of cognitive development. Vygotsky stated that children are born with "elementary mental functions," which he defined as "fundamental skills for intellectual development." Vygotsky, like Piaget, believes that young children are naturally curious and actively involved in their own learning, as well as the discovery and development of new knowledge.

MORAL DEVELOPMENT

The psychology study of moral growth has grown significantly, both in terms of theoretical diversity and in terms of the number of theoretical viewpoints represented in the area. Children form configurations of thinking about welfare, justice, and rights linked to feelings like attachment, sympathy, and empathy, according to a structural developmental relational perspective. Children form systems of judgements in the domains of social convention, which include uniformities within social systems, and the personal domain, which involves understandings of permissible realms of choice, freedoms, and autonomy, in addition to moral judgments. Moral, conventional, and personal judgments are unique from one another in this social domain approach, and they form separate growth trajectories. Adulthood phases for moral growth are discussed after evaluating the qualities of the cognitive-developmental stage concept, which has previously been limited in its application to child and adolescent development. Other approaches to moral formation and accompanying basic psychological assumptions are compared to the structural relational domain approach. From birth through adulthood, moral development is concerned with the emergence, change, and comprehension of morality.

Morality develops during the course of a person's life and is influenced by their experiences and conduct when confronted with moral concerns at various stages of physical and cognitive development. In summary, morality is concerned with an individual's developing sense of what is good and wrong; as a result, young children's moral judgement and character differ from that of an adult. Morality is frequently used interchangeably with the terms "rightness" and "goodness." It refers to a code of conduct that guides one's activities, behaviours, and beliefs and is drawn from one's culture, religion, or personal philosophy.

LAWRENCE KOHLBERG

educationaltechnology.net

Lawrence Kohlberg was an American psychologist who is best known for his moral development phases theory. He devised a research programme to better understand moral development—which he referred to as justice development—over the course of a lifetime. Kohlberg investigated the stage of development and moral perspectives of children, adolescents, and adults in the United States and overseas using dilemma interviews and a detailed scoring manual. He talked about the relationship between judgement and action, the transnational universality of moral development, and gender-related morality in this context. His groundbreaking interdisciplinary work spanned subjects as diverse as developmental psychology, philosophy, and education, to name a few. His study was inspirational in many ways and will continue to be inspirational for years to come. Lawrence Kohlberg has been advancing his cognitive development hypothesis of moralization, which has become prominent in the study of moral development and its application to moral education, for nearly three decades. Kohlberg's moral development theory is concerned with how children learn morality and moral reasoning. According to Kohlberg's thesis, moral development develops in six stages.

The theory also suggests that moral logic is primarily focused on seeking and maintaining justice. Each stage offers a new perspective, but not everyone functions at the highest level all the time. There were three levels of moral reasoning that encompassed the six stages. The three levels were Pre-Conventional, Conventional and post conventional. The six stages are:

Stage 1: The first stage emphasizes children's self-interest in decision-making as they try to avoid punishment at all costs. Kohlberg considers children's moral thinking. They believe that regulations are expected to be observed at a young age, and that people in control will definitely punish them.

Stage 2: This stage examines how youngsters learn to embrace the viewpoints taught, while simultaneously acknowledging that there are several points of view on each topic. Each person is unique and, as a result, will have a distinct perspective based on their interests.

Stage 3: This stage acknowledges the desire to be accepted into societal groupings, as well as how the outcome affects each individual.

Stage 4: Laws and social order are supreme at this point. It is necessary to follow and obey the rules and regulations. Stage four depicts a person's moral growth as a member of a larger society. Everyone becomes more conscious of how their activities affect others and concentrates on their own position, following rules, and respecting authorities.

Stage 5: This stage acknowledges the introduction of abstract reasoning as people attempt to explain specific behaviors.

Stage 6: Moral reasoning is founded on personal values, according to the final step of Kohlberg's theory. When Kohlberg recognised that elected methods do not always provide fair outcomes, he created Stage 6. To acknowledge the application of justice in moral thinking, the sixth stage was formed. As a starting point for what is good and just, general, universal morality and ethics are applied. These are frequently abstract concepts that can only be sketched rather than defined. Universal principles are based on values like equality, fairness, dignity, and respect.

CONCLUSION

According to Kohlberg's findings, each stage of moral development occurs one at a time and in the same order. Moral growth is invariant; individuals progress through the phases one at a time and in a predetermined order, but some may never reach the ultimate level. He also came to the conclusion that the stages' order is universal across all cultures.

REFERENCES

- Tudge, J., & Rogoff, B. (1999). Peer influences on cognitive development: Piagetian and Vygotskian perspectives. Lev Vygotsky: critical assessments, 3, 32-56.
- Mandler, J. M. (1990). A new perspective on cognitive development in infancy. American Scientist, 78(3), 236-243.
- Takaya, K. (2008). Jerome Bruner's theory of education: From early Bruner to later Bruner. Interchange, 39(1), 1-19.
- Astington, J. W., & Olson, D. R. (1995). The cognitive revolution in children's understanding of mind. Human development, 38(4-5), 179-189.
- Huitt, W., & Hummel, J. (2003). Piaget's theory of cognitive development. Educational psychology interactive, 3(2), 1-5.
- McLeod, S. A. (2014). Lev vygotsky.
- Piaget, J. (1965). The moral development. New York: Free Press, 1(1), 0.
- Turiel, E. (2015). Moral development. Handbook of child psychology and developmental science, 1-39.
- Kohlberg, L. (1986). Lawrence Kohlberg, consensus and controversy (No. 1). Routledge.

CHAPTER XVII

ADJUSTMENT CONCEPT AND DEFENCE MECHANISM

Dr Abhishek Srivastava, Associate Professor, Faculty of Management Studies,
Gopal Narayan Singh University, Rohtas, Bihar.

• • •

Introduction

In science, adjustment refers to the activity method in that humans and alternative animals accomplish a balance between their various needs or between their demands and therefore the difficulties in their circumstances. Once a necessity is felt, a series of changes begins and finishes with the satisfaction of that requirement. Hungry folks, for example, are compelled to hunt food by their state. They're acclimated to the current explicit demand after they eat as a result of the stimulating scenario that compelled them to action is reduced after they eat.

What is an adjustment?

The word "adjustment" comes from the word "adaptation" in biology. Biologists used the phrase "adaptation" to discuss changes within the physical demands of the surroundings, whereas psychologists use the term "adjustment" to discuss with changes within the social or interpersonal relationships in society.

The individual's response to the stress and pressures of the social surroundings is noted as adjustment. The individual could also be needed to retort to associate external or internal demand.

The adjustment has been seen by psychologists from 2 perspectives: "adjustment as a goal" and "adjustment as a method."

Adjustment as an achievement:

The term "adjustment as an achievement" refers to a human ability to fulfil his job effectively in a very style of things. If we tend to contemplate adjustment to be a hit, we tend to should establish criteria to assess the standard of the adjustment. Psychologists have developed four criteria for judging the adequacy of adjustment. the subsequent are a number of them:

- Physical well-being
- Psychological ease
- Efficiency within the work and
- Acceptance in society
- Adjustment as a process:

The phrase "adjustment as a process" emphasises the method by that an individual adjusts to his or her surroundings. It's essential, significantly from the attitude of academics. The degree to that students change is primarily determined by their interactions with the surroundings in which they live. They're perpetually trying to adapt to that. Jean Piaget checked out the adaptive method from a spread of views.

Assimilation and accommodation are terms utilized by Jean Piaget to explain the method of adjusting oneself or one's surroundings.

An assimilator could be one who retains his or her principles and standards of conduct no matter the massive changes within the social atmosphere.

The term "accommodator" refers to somebody WHO adapts their concepts to the dynamic ideals of society by taking their standards from their social setting.

In order to with success integrate into society, an individual should use each device, specifically assimilation and accommodation.

Characteristics of a well-adjusted person:

Some noticeable activity patterns ought to be a gift in a very healthy and well-balanced person. These patterns of behaviour should be according to human social expectations. the subsequent are some samples of these patterns:

- Imaginative maturity
- Emotional equilibrium
- Others are treated with heat and thought.
- Free from the strain of everyday occurrences
- Making selections on your own
- Elements in adjustment:
- There are many key factors for meeting the wants that ar needed for a human healthy adjustment. the subsequent are the details:
- Satisfaction of necessities
- There is no impediment to meeting desires.

- Strong motivations for meeting demands
- Possibility of appropriate geographical surroundings to satisfy desires

Mechanisms of adjustment

Individuals use 'adjustment mechanisms' to regulate their surroundings, solve difficulties, and touch upon the anxiety-inducing and conflicting processes of life. Any habitual strategy of overcoming blockages, accomplishing goals, satisfying reasons, easing frustration, and associated conserving physiological conditions will be classified as an adjustment mechanism. Every person depends on his or her own mechanisms to stay balanced in his or her adjustment at intervals and toward a society under control.

Defence mechanism

Any of a group of mental processes that allows the mind to succeed in compromise solutions to disputes that it's unable to resolve, in keeping with psychotherapy theory. The compromise is sometimes unconscious, and it entails the concealment of internal urges or sensations that threaten to undermine shallowness or cause anxiety in oneself. the thought is predicated on the psychotherapy theory that there square measure opposing forces within the mind that fight one different. Sigmund Freud coined the term in his study "The Neuro-Psychoses of Defense" (1894).

The following square measure a number of the main defence mechanisms delineated by psychoanalysts:

1. Repression is the method of golf stroke associates degree unwelcome plan, affect, or need into the unconscious space of the mind so as to get rid of it from consciousness. An instance of a hysterical cognitive state, within which the victim performs or witnesses a terrible act and later on entirely forgets concerning it and therefore the circumstances encompassing it, is an associate degree example.

2. Reaction creation is the acutely aware concentration on associate degree opposing thought, mood, or need to a feared unconscious impulse. as an example, a mother World Health Organization bears associate degree unwanted child might react to her guilt for not needing the kid by changing into protective and solicitous so as to steer each the kid and herself that she could be a smart mother.

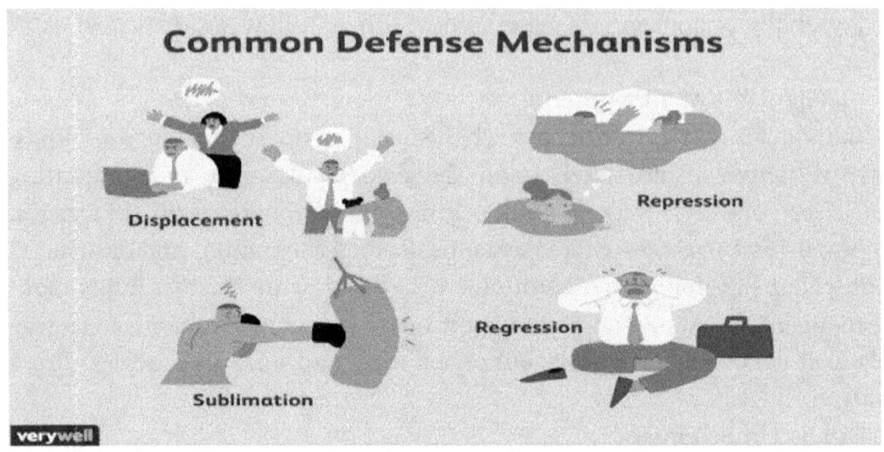

Source: very well

3. Projection could be a protection mechanism within which unsought sentiments square measure projected onto another person, wherever they're perceived as a danger from the surface world. once a private is intimidated by his own furious feelings, he accuses another of harbouring hostile concepts, that could be a common sort of projection.

4. Regression could be a comeback to earlier stages of development and abandoned forms of pleasure that square measure related to them, triggered by dangers or conflicts that arise at one in all the later stages.

After her first dispute with her husband, a young wife can retire to the safety of her parents' house.

5. Sublimation is the redirection of instinctive desires, usually sexual ones, into non-instinctual channels. According to psychoanalytic thought, the energy spent on sexual desires can be diverted to more socially acceptable and even productive pursuits, such as artistic or scientific endeavours.

6. Denial is the deliberate reluctance to acknowledge the existence of uncomfortable realities. An individual can avoid intolerable ideas, feelings, or experiences by suppressing hidden feelings of homosexuality or animosity, or mental problems in one's child.

The deployment of a defence mechanism is a normal element of personality function, according to psychoanalysts, and is not an indication of psychiatric disease in and of itself. Excessive or strict employment of these defences, on the other hand, can be a symptom of a variety of psychological illnesses.

CONCLUSION

For one thing, adjustment is a goal, and for another, it is a process. The first highlights the effectiveness or quality of adjustment, while the second emphasises the process by which an individual adjusts to his external environment. Thus, healthy adjustment is a process in which an individual successfully achieves his biological, psychological, and social requirements while also establishing a balance between his inner wants and society's outward demands through appropriate behavioural reactions.

REFERENCES

- https://www.britannica.com/science/photoperiodism
- http://www.edugyan.in/2017/03/adjustment-maladjustment.html
- https://www.britannica.com/topic/defense-mechanism
- esearchgate.net/publication/ 314087231_ADJUSTMENT_PROCESS_ACHEIVEMENT_
- CHARACTERISTICS_MEASUREMENT_AND_DIMENSIONS
- http://egyankosh.ac.in/bitstream/123456789/8519/1/Unit-16.pdf
- https://www.indiastudychannel.com/resources/131499-Types-of-adjustment-in-Psychology.aspx
- https://dictionary.apa.org/adjustment
- https://en.wikipedia.org/wiki/Adjustment_(psychology)
- https://www.simplypsychology.org/defense-mechanisms.html
- https://nptel.ac.in/content/storage2/courses/109104070/ Module-1.pdf

CHAPTER XVIII

BANDURA'S THEORY OF SOCIAL LEARNING

Divine Tomar, Pupil Teacher, Manvi Institute of Education andTechnology, SCERT, Delhi.
Mr.Anand Prakash Dube,Associate Professor, School of Management Sciences, Varanasi.

● ● ●

Introduction

Albert Bandura was a Canadian-American psychologist and the David Starr Jordan Professor of Psychology at Stanford University. He was born in Mundare, Alberta, a small town with about 400 residents, as the youngest and only son of a family of six. In addition to his contributions to personality psychology, social cognitive theory, therapy, and other areas of psychology, Bandura also had a significant impact on the shift from behaviorism to cognitive psychology. He is credited with creating the bleeding' theoretical notion and the social learning theory, which has since been called the social cognitive theory. Due to this subpar academic setting, Bandura quickly understood that learning is mostly a social and self-directed activity. In his words, "the instruments of self-directedness serve one well over this, but the content of most textbooks is perishable. He is one of the psychologists who has been referenced the most often throughout history, frequently being likened to Skinner, Freud, and Piaget in terms of importance. His social cognitive theory of human functioning, which places a strong emphasis on an agentic perspective on self-development, adaptation, and change, has had a profound impact on psychology, revolutionizing theories of behavior change and influencing education, public health, parenting, clinical health practice, and governmental policy. In 1974, when the American Psychological Association (APA) was suffering financial cuts from the Nixon government and bad press regarding the risks of behavior modification, he served as its president. He oversaw the Association for the Advancement of Psychology's foundation because he saw it as a means of applying psychological science to the creation of public policy. On July 26, 2021, Bandura passed away in his home. Albert Bandura's social learning theory places a strong emphasis on the value of seeing, modelling, and copying other people's behaviors, attitudes, and emotional responses. The interaction of environmental and cognitive influences on human cognition and behavior is taken into account by the social learning hypothesis. Albert Bandura (1977) concurs with the behaviorist learning theories of classical conditioning and operant conditioning in terms of social learning theory.

Source: www.verywellmind.com

SLT is frequently referred to as the "bridge" between the cognitive approach and conventional learning theory (i.e., behaviorism). This is due to the fact that it emphasizes the role that mental (cognitive) variables have in learning. Contrary to Skinner, Bandura (1977) thinks that people actively digest information and consider the connection between their actions and the results. Nabavi (2014) claims that Bandura carried out his well-known experiment, also known as the Bobo doll experiment, in 1961 to analyze behavioral patterns and test the social learning hypothesis, which holds that people learn similar behaviors by modelling their own behavior after the acts of role models. Bandura's findings from the Bobo Doll Experiment altered the direction of modern psychology and are largely recognized with influencing the move away from pure behaviorism and toward cognitive psychology in academia. He showed how youngsters pick up on and copy actions they see in other individuals. Bandura argued that not all types of learning could be accounted for by direct reinforcement and that people may pick up new knowledge and behaviors by observing other people, according to Banyard & Grayson (2000). The ability of learners to absorb and exhibit the behaviors demonstrated in their surroundings is the subject of social learning theories. Children are surrounded by many powerful role models in society, including their parents, other family members, people they see on television or in social media, their friends from their peer group, their religion, other people in the community, and their school. Children observe some of these socialization agents and adopt the behaviors they display. Even if the behavior is inappropriate, children may imitate it later on. However, there are several factors that increase the likelihood that a child will imitate the behavior that its society views as appropriate for its sex and age.

Significance of Social Learning theories

The teachers' personality through a process of social learning has important influence on students' behavior and efficiency of the educational process and that the various development and educational programs aimed at the teachers' empowerment and encouraging the operation of positive social impact, can significantly contribute to the quality and improvement of the effects of the educational efforts on the school and preschool age. Understanding how and why people develop emotional ties, take on gender roles, establish friends, pick up moral values, and change in countless other ways is the focus of social learning theories. The educational process in the modern era is becoming more and more complicated, influenced by several intrapersonal and interpersonal aspects. The social learning theory of Bandura, which emphasizes the value of so-called social learning, or learning by model, when situated in an educational context, serves as the conceptual underpinning of this study. It's unclear how the topic of visual culture relates to the social learning hypothesis, which claims that learning happens through observation in social environments. These two concepts' theoretical relationship was contested. It was observed that there are linkages between the experiences people have as a result of their daily interactions with visual cultural forms and social learning. It was discovered that visual culture forms allow viewers who are prone to watch and mimic actions with model characteristics to live vicariously through them. It has been discovered that the livings—acquired observant learning from visual culture forms—shape people's attitudes and behaviors. According to the study, looking at visual culture as an environmental factor in the context of social learning will help to comprehend and shed light on the changing, transforming, and emerging aspects of human behavior in the twenty-first century. Albert Bandura is credited with initially introducing the self-efficacy construct. According to Bandura (1986), dealing with one's surroundings entails a complicated collection of activities. To exert some influence over events that have an impact on people's lives, cognitive, social, and behavioral subskills must be arranged into integrated action plans. Bandura's notion that the efficient use and execution of these subskills are significantly tied to people's beliefs of their own efficacy in using these skills is confirmed by an expanding number of research findings from many domains. According to Bandura, the fundamental tenet of the self-efficacy theory is that an individual's expectations for success (outcome expectations) and personal mastery (efficacy expectations) decide whether they would engage in a certain behavior. These two types of expectations, efficacy expectations and outcome expectations, together with a person's qualities, conduct, and results of behavior, make up Bandura's model of self-efficacy theory. A person's conviction about the results that follow from a specific behavior is known as an outcome expectation. These consequences may be physical, social, or self-evaluative in nature. A self-efficacy expectation, also known as an efficacy expectation, is the belief in one's ability to carry out the behavior. People are driven to act in ways they think will lead to the results they want. However, self-efficacy predicts performance considerably better than expected outcomes since efficacy expectations (self-efficacy) are significantly correlated with outcome expectations. He questioned the ideas that were prevalent at the time about learning and education. By doing this, he made a substantial contribution to our understanding of early childhood development and learning. Perhaps Bandura's most famous theory is his "social learning theory," which he renamed "social cognitive theory" in 1986 to reflect what he believed to be the much larger and more complicated structure of children's thinking and how they learnt. Where a doll like that was. As they had seen the woman do in the movie, the kids began to hit the doll. They were essentially copying the woman's behavior.

The Bobo Doll Experiment

Children were exposed to two separate adult models for the experiment: an aggressive model and a non-aggressive one. Following the observation of the adult's behavior, the kids would be put in a room without the model and watched to see if they would replicate the actions they had earlier seen. Boys would behave more aggressively than girls, children would imitate models of the same sex rather than models of the opposite sex, and children who witnessed an adult acting aggressively would be likely to act aggressively even when the adult model was not present, were just a few of Bandura's key predictions about what would happen during the Bobo doll experiment. In his well-known experiment with the Bobo doll, Bandura proved that kids pick up on and replicate actions they see in other people. In Bandura's studies, kids saw an adult behave irrationally toward a Bobo doll. Later, when the kids were permitted to play with the Bobo doll in a room, they started acting aggressively just like they had before. First, a child that feels itself as similar to others is more inclined to pay attention to and copy them. Second, the child will either receive reinforcement for the imitation behavior from those around them or punishment. If a youngster imitates a model's conduct and the results are pleasing, the child is probably going to keep acting in the same way. Third, when considering whether or not to mimic someone's actions, the youngster will also consider what happens to other individuals. A person gains knowledge by seeing how their actions affect others. The experiment, in the opinion of Bandura and his coworkers, shows how particular behaviors can be acquired through imitation and observation. According to Bandura, youngsters came to feel that such violence was appropriate due to the adult models' violent behavior toward the dolls. He added that as a result, kids might be more likely to act violently when they are frustrated in the future.

Source: https://m.facebook.com

Criticisms

One of the most well-known research in psychology is still Bandura's experiment. Social psychologists are still investigating how violence in the media affects children's behavior today. It did, however, come under some criticism. Some detractors claim that the experiment's findings may not be representative of what happens in the real world because it was conducted in a lab setting. Additionally, it has been proposed that youngsters may have merely been trying to appease the adults when they smacked the Bobo doll, rather than being motivated to act aggressively. Some critics argue that the study itself was unethical. By manipulating the children into behaving aggressively, they argue, the experimenters were essentially teaching the children to be aggressive. The study might suffer from selection bias. All participants were drawn from a narrow pool of students who share the same racial and socioeconomic background. This makes it difficult to generalize the results to a larger, more diverse population.

Conclusion

If people had to only learn from the results of their own acts, it would be extremely difficult to learn, not to mention dangerous. Fortunately, the majority of human behavior is acquired by modelling and observation: through watching others, one develops an understanding of how new behaviors are carried out, and this coded information later on acts as a guide for action. A normative objective in natural resource management and policy is social learning. Regarding its theoretical underpinnings or meaning, there is still some disagreement. There is frequently little separation between individual and broader social learning, and social learning is sometimes confused with other ideas like participation and proenvironmental conduct. There are many unproven claims about social learning, and the idea itself and its potential effects are commonly misunderstood. Our ability to determine whether social learning has taken place, and if so, what kind of learning has taken place, to what extent, between whom, when, and how, has been hampered by this lack of conceptual clarity.

REFERENCES

- McLeod, S. (2011). Albert Bandura's social learning theory.
- Bandura, A., & Evans, R. I. (2006). Albert Bandura. Insight Media.
- Artino Jr, A. R. (2007). Bandura, Ross, and Ross: Observational Learning and the Bobo Doll. Online submission.
- Edinyang, S. D. (2016). The significance of social learning theories in the teaching of social studies education. International Journal of Sociology and Anthropology Research, 2(1), 40-45.
- Marić, M., Sakač, M., Lipovac, V., Nikolić, S., Raičević, J., & Saračević, M. (2017). Teachers and social lcarning as a factor of modern educational competencies. Bulgarian Journal of Science and Education Policy, 11(2), 233-245.
- Yılmaz, M., Yılmaz, U., & Yılmaz, E. N. D. (2019). The relation between social learning and visual culture. International Electronic Journal of Elementary Education, 11(4), 421-427.
- Shortridge-Baggett, L. M. (2000). The theory and measurement of the self-efficacy construct. Self-efficacy in nursing: Research and

measurement perspectives, 9-28.

- Bandura, A., & Hall, P. (2018). Albert bandura and social learning theory. Learning theories for early years practice, 63.
- Cherry, K., & Swaim, E. (2020). What the Bobo Doll Experiment reveals about kids and aggression.
- Ozer, E. M. (2022). Albert Bandura (1925–2021).
- Reed, M. S., Evely, A. C., Cundill, G., Fazey, I., Glass, J., Laing, A., ... & Stringer, L. C. (2010). What is social learning?. Ecology and society, 15(4).
- Cherry, K. (2012). Social learning theory. Retrieved July, 2, 2012.

CHAPTER XIX

CREATIVITY'S INVENTION

Krittibas Datta,State Aided College Teacher,Department of Political Science,
Jalangi Mahavidyalaya, Murshidabad,West Bengal, India.

• • •

INTRODUCTION

Creativity and Innovation are traits that people strive to cultivate in order to help them see the world in new ways and form ideas to improve or add to it. They are active characteristics, which means they must be used intentionally in order to produce something beneficial or authentic. Creativity is used to express an idea or concept, whereas innovation is used to solve a problem.

What exactly are creativity and innovation?

Creativity is not a genetic trait; rather, it develops as a person continues to learn and grow, and uses their imagination for various forms of expression. Creativity has no intrinsic value unless it is manifested into reality.

The process of taking creative ideas and turning them into commercial and financial success is known as innovation. An innovator's creation is an innovation. Because innovation is the application of creative ideas, it is inherently linked to creativity, and the two work in tandem. A physical object or a concept to improve or create a new process can both be considered innovations. People innovate to solve problems or make society more functional.

Creativity and innovation are important because they enable the world to cvolve, grow, and change over time. Innovation cannot occur without creativity, and creativity is insignificant if not applied. They are both essential to the progression and advancement of human civilization as people consider new ways to express their ideas and develop those ideas into innovations that make society safer, healthier, and more accessible. Creativity and innovation have benefited society by giving birth to: Medicine \Music \Communication \Transportation \Art

Creativity occurs when people use their imagination to generate new ideas, solve problems, and consider possibilities that no one else has considered. The scope of one's creativity is only limited by one's ability to think outside the box. Because of the nature of creativity, the creation of an idea is unique and original to the creative thinker.Creativity is increasingly cited as the key to social and economic change in the twenty-first century. It is also a very modern concept—making its first appearance as an English noun in 1875. This essay investigates the cultural construction of creativity in the context of the history of ideas. It understands creativity not as an innate human instinct or ability, but as an idea that emerges out of specific historical moments, shaped by the discourses of politics, science, commerce, and nation. It shifts the ground of analysis away from the naturalized models that have traditionally dominated the field of creative practice research, in order to highlight the historicity of a concept that is more commonly deemed to be without history.

Source: https://axiomq.com/

The investigations show if artists confronting substantial external limitations in their creativeness vary from artists who are free to decide on the subjects and resources, the time schedule, and so on in their notions of creation. Sixty-four artists from various fields of visual art have provided free definitions of creativity and classified the quality of products and individuals as characteristic of their unique creative definitions. As a control group were included 47 psychology students. Contents analyses of the free definitions and quantitative analysis of the classifications both revealed systematic distinctions between 'free' artists (for example painters or sculptors), more restricted artists (such as architects and designers), and psychological pupils. The one thing accepted by all the groups was for a creative individual to have numerous ideas. For example, we discovered disparity in terms of the relevance of a job for a creative product or the importance of a creative person's capacity to solve difficulties. Psychology students tended to highlight good sentiments produced by creative activity, although creativity was commonly called a hard effort for both groups of artists.

This section examines the subject of creativity in the artificial intelligence area (AI). Besides the uncertainties with respect to product, method or person, for four reasons, the definition of creativity is challenging. The first issue is that the notion requires a positive assessment. An concept that is considered innovative needs to be intriguing. This assessment typically relies on the variables of society and history and these assessments cannot be explained solely by psychological theory. The second issue is whether the author has to realise the worth of an idea to be referred to as creative. If so, someone with a good idea but who rejects it is not innovative. The third problem is the strain between historical (H) and psychological (P) sentiments. An thought is creative if it is innovative, even if others have previously had this concept in regard of the intellect. An concept is H-creative when it's P-creative and nobody has ever had the notion. Creativity with H is more glamorous, while creativity with P is more essential. The fourth difficulty is that only a few instances are covered by the usual operational definition. Many psychologists characterize the unique synthesis of common concepts as creativity. This is neither a distinction between P-News and H-News or an assessment. Two definitions of creativity are therefore needed, both of which need an intriguing new concept. The creativity of improbability involves new and unlikely pairings of old concepts. Novel thoughts that the individual could not have had before regarding the current domain conventions relate to the impossibility or exploratory-transformation creativity. These two creative kinds are described in this chapter and AI models are discussed in relation to arts and science.

While creativity may enhance the unity of approach only as a uniqueness, usefulness and surprise, the same definition shows that creativity can diminish in seven distinct ways. These options have been recognized :

(a) fortunate bias in response,

(b) irrational perseverance;

(c) problem discovery;

(d) rational removal,

(e) irrational removing; and

(f) blissful ignorance. Routine or reproductive or customable concepts.

In addition to giving a more detailed understanding of creative failure, the term has important implications for the processes and processes necessary to create highly innovative ideas.

CONCEPT OF CREATIVITY

Source: https://static3.depositphotos.com/

In all parts of life, creativity is an important idea, because creative individuals assure development. However, a strong definition of creativity is still lacking. This was not a significant concern in the 1950s since creative research was restricted to creative individuality and the process of creative thinking. As the 20th century proceeded, the study area was divided and a broad range of definitions of creativity were established. As a single definition is required for practical study into a concept, a new examination of the idea of creativity has to be undertaken in the 21st century. Creativity is an important notion in all areas of life since creative people ensure growth. However, there is currently no solid definition of creativity. This was not relevant in the 1950s, since creative study was limited to creative uniqueness and the creative thought process. With the course of the 20th century, the subject of research was separated and a wide variety of creativity definitions were defined. A new inquiry into the idea of creativity must be done in the 21st century since a single definition is needed for a concrete research on a topic. Every word supplied as a response was considered to have a significant connection with creativity both in the first and second studies. The outcome was a 42-word list. In the third and most significant research, the remaining 42 words were split into groups or categories by a fresh set of students. The card-sorting approach was used: Each participant was given 42 words in individual cards, which he was instructed to sort in groups. The rationale for the categorization was deliberately kept unclear, so the participants had to name the groups. This approach has often included certain terms whilst no participants have put other words together. The more often they put together two terms, the deeper the connection between them. An analysis of the Hierarchical Cluster was used to disclose the strengths of all these linkages. This might lead to the formation of groupings of words. The eight components of creativity provide the most essential conclusion to this theory. A comparison analysis using a different measurement technique of association strength was carried out to check the outcomes of the investigations. This study demonstrated that the varied ways of evaluating the strengths of the connection were unexpectedly unlike many. The discussion section provides possible causes for this difference. In naming the creativity components, the conclusion of the thesis may be demonstrated: - Originality - Emotion - Inventiveness - Process - Intellectuality - Hobby - Practice.

In this article, two corporations of the literature examine recent research on the notion of creativity in two cultures—the Eastern (Asian) cultures and the Western (European and US). One is on people's implied creativity theories via different cultures and the other about cross-cultural creativity research. Studies on implicit creative ideas in the East reveal that many Asians have many individuals in the West who have similar but not identical views of creativity. Cross-cultural creativity research indicate that East and West differ in their differing thought and creative manifestations on average. It presents a concept of creativity as largely culture-specific and discusses the suitability of utilizing diverging thought tests to assess creativity.

The idea of creativity is challenged for being too loosely defined and overly influenced by an operationalist approach from below. It is also said that current popular creative definitions do not separate creativity from traditional concepts of intelligence, which likewise rely on novelty and adequacy as essential characteristics, by emphasizing on originality and suitability.

This conceptual issue is solved by clearly distinguishing the novelty on the stimulus from the novelty on the response side. This distinction is utilized as a foundation to create a new taxonomy of creativity and intelligent behavior of different sorts. The difference between proactive and reactive creativity is an important characteristic of this new approach. In conclusion, the conceptual model is utilized to identify some deficiencies in existing creative tests and to provide certain proposals with regard to the architecture of a new type of creativity evaluation taking account of a practical-educational viewpoint.

Proposes that validation of the idea of an ordinarily distributed characteristic for creativity should be positively linked in unselected samples to traits that separate famous creatives from less eminent individuals. The notion is not clearly supported by an assessment of the existing evidence. Taken along with previous data, this finding shows that a divergent thought should not be considered creative. Discuss creativity as a voyage since it needs attention and may involve key moments that disturb or discontinue creativity. The creative path has 7 processes: framing, testing, explore, revalue, reinforce, reframe and realize. In every step there is a shift in the connection of the pursuer to the phenomena and fresh perspectives are obtained.

PROCESS OF CREATIVITY

Source: https://image.shutterstock.com/

At least four components are creativity:

(1) creative output,

(2) creative individual and

(3) creative scenario

(4) creation output;

Theoretical views, each having its own assumptions, methods, biases, and even meta-theory perspectives have been examined from so many sometimes-contradictory angles that it is not feasible to address all in one chapter. This chapter focuses on the divergent approach to the analysis of the creative process, which has the best theoretical basis, most creativity tests and the most empirical research. In addition, information will be given on some additional components and theoretical methods. Creativity in various fields is seen in different ways: it is referred to as 'innovation' in education, 'entrepreneurship' in business, typically referred to as 'problem solving' in mathematics and 'performance' or 'composition' in music. A creative output in diverse fields with its own laws, techniques and concepts of creativity are assessed against the standards of that domain.

Learning, however, is made of both product and process in every academic area. Although in many fields the output might be fairly diverse, there are common pedagogical concepts that promote process creativity. 'Creative teaching' might be called the creation of a learning environment that encourages students to see both the essence and the subject details, to formulate and resolve problems, to look at the connectivity between different fields, to take up and to respond to new ideas and to include the element of surprise in their work. Such a learning environment includes not just suitable resources, but also learning approaches that address the crucial emotive elements of creativity.

Her goods have been the most popular method of detecting creativity. The presence of a creative output is a precondition for considering creativity in architecture, music, literature, art, even problem resolving and scientific discovery. Alternatively, anecdotal accounts were utilized to identify creative processes. Many scientific findings have been associated with an unexplained insight or revelation, marked by the AHA! Response. Apart from the creative output itself and the answer from AHA! There are several forms of physical proof that show the creative process. Our objective is to study these phenomenon's further and to create ideas on the nature of the creative process. Our ultimate objective is to build a broad creativity theory. This idea is based on the circumstances needed for the creative process in a variety of fields: riddles, scientific discoveries, design with a particular focus on architectural design.

Hypothesizes that creative activity is a particular way of connecting the primary and secundary processes, in which the loose, illogical and highly subjective concept of the primary process generates a new thought or insight. This is then shaped into a setting that is socially relevant and relevant to others through a subsequent process. Although evidence of creativity is poor by the degree of primary process involvement reveals how creative capabilities connect to the extent to which the secondary process starts integrative control over the manifestations of primary processes. There is a discussion about the difference between science and art. It is also described how certain creative styles may depend on the direct access to primary-process thought by the secondary process, while other styles may entail the usage in creation of particular functions from the secondary process.

ROLE OF SCHOOL IN FOSTERING CREATIVITY

Source: https://centaur-wp.s3.eu-central-1.amazonaws.com/

Despite composition's inclusion in music curriculum in the UK, USA, Canada and Australia, it remains a fragmented and challenging problem to grasp the function of creativity for composing in schools. The purpose of this article is to rely on an international understanding of the makeup of individual pupils from different origins. This research is aimed at developing instructional techniques that may encourage creativity during composition. Over the last five years, the focus for policymakers in education has been on innovation. However, there has been an upsurge in interest in creativity, with no relation to the value system. This essay contends that Western individualism, in turn, supported as well as led by the worldwide capitalist market, really supplied an unseen underlying value framework. What may this imply to promote creativity in classrooms with wisdom?

This book provides more inspirational insight and encourages instructors to appreciate a more diverse array of abilities, with special emphasis on creativity, novelty, discovery and so on. Techniques and methods are proposed in the classroom to promote risky and innovative thinking. It is also, and maybe particularly crucial for creativity, important that teachers be clear in understanding the emotional and motivational foundation of learning and thinking to focus on its cognitive components not simply. Therefore the book is anticipated that the vast variety of elements in the classroom that influence conventional as well as creative thinking will be more fully understood.

Initially, education concerns drive the increase in interest in creativity after the Sputnik shock in the 1950s. These focused on the notion that schools and colleges produced huge numbers of graduates, but most of them were educated to use the traditional methods previously known. The proposal that features required for creativity are helpful to develop by providing adequate learning environments deliberately supports creativity in schools.

This chapter focuses on identifying what instructors should encourage and use concepts for this purpose. Two Many instructors and parents are uncomfortable with the emphasis on school creativity since that may encourage disobedience, disobedience, carefree conduct or just uncertainty. Others perceive a demand for innovation in the classroom to be permitted by any behavior and forsake essential skills, norms, and principles such as right or wrong. All children and young people experience the processes and personal properties involved in promoting creativity in the lesson and promoting creativity helps all pupils, not only the handful that are renewed as renowned innovators. From the beginning we should also realise that the aim to encourage creativeness is an integral element of an educational heritage which goes back to ancient Greeks at least.

Many creative training methods appear to only increase performance for activities directly related to training. Rump (1979) found in a thorough examination on data that, when the criteria closely match the training process, the impact of training is highest and worst when this resemblance is modest. Only limited impacts (as opposed to thinking) are achieved in the case of personalities, interests and preferences. As a result, it may be concluded that training processes affect attitudes, values, self-image or motivation minimally. It is also possible to have a contrary impact from the targeted creative education. For example, students could become aware that some types of conduct are favored by the instructor and that the teacher could change his/her approach to issues appropriately. While the education can motivate youngsters to work hard on many tasks, they can learn that "original" responses are easily provided by division of hair, ranging replies without regard to correctness or relevancy, or delivering surprising tricks. The creative process does not depend on any unique abilities, which can be acquired in math like tables, in much the same manner that specialist bodybuilding can be created. What is necessary is to promote creativity through specific techniques of teaching and learning spread over the full curriculum.

WHAT SHOULD TEACHERS FOSTER?

Source: https://static.babyandchild.ae/

Early creativity studies mostly focused on creative thought (see specifics later). It became abundantly obvious, however, that kids show only inventiveness if and when they choose to. In addition, youngsters must be able to identify discrepancies and generate suggestions, for example. The subsequent parts will examine these characteristics of creativity in greater depth. The key components of this constellation need to be outlined at that time, as these are the processes and qualities that instructors must encourage in the classroom to foster creative development. Learners should regard the collection of knowledge, certain methods of thinking, inventiveness in discovering answers, the capacity to assess ideas, the ability to convey solutions to other people and the evaluation of real-world solutions as fundamental components of creativity. Taylor (1975) 9 also gave insights on the distinction between truly (the actually startling) creative and other types of novelty. Five degrees of creativity were described:

(a) technical creativity is seen with exceptional linguistics, tools, tools of trade, tools and such like,

(b) inventive creativity involves using in an innovative fashion what has been known;

(c) innovative creativity takes place where known principles or paradigms are employed to develop new ideas; and

(d) emergent creativity; and

(e) innovative creativity;

Dillon (1982) indicates that there are three challenges:

(a) identification of evident problems on the basis of field knowledge;

(b) identification of hidden difficulties on the basis of concentrated effort in the area; and

(c) inventing problems because existing information is reorganized.

Teachers are familiar with defining the difficulties students are faced with and assessing to what degree the answers of students match with the proper answer that is commonly known to the teacher in advance. Convergent thinking is applying conventional logic to a number of information components in order to include the one and only optimal solution suggested by the information available—the response which would have come from anyone who had the same stock and who applied the principles of conventional logic. Since the solution is unique and develops more or less unavoidably from the information given, it already exists and should only be discovered in a particular sense. Divergent thought, on the other hand, entails answering by deviating, for example, from the given knowledge, by perceiving unforeseen elements that other people could not see. Knowledge in the field is the reason for recognizing such gaps (Birch, 1975). The following summarizes the results of this study on the cognitive elements of creativity for teachers. In their pupils they should aim to promote:

1 Fund of general knowledge possession.

2 One or more particular areas of knowledge.

3 An active imagination.

4 Ability to identify, find or invent issues.

5 Ability to recognize linkages, overlaps, parallels, and logical consequences (convergent thinking).

6. Competency to create distant relationships, to combine, to accept main process material, to create new designs, etc. (divergent thinking).

7. Ability to find several solutions to issues.

8. A lodging choice, not assimilation

9. Capacity to share results with other people.

10. Ability and desire to review their own work.

FOSTERING CREATIVITY

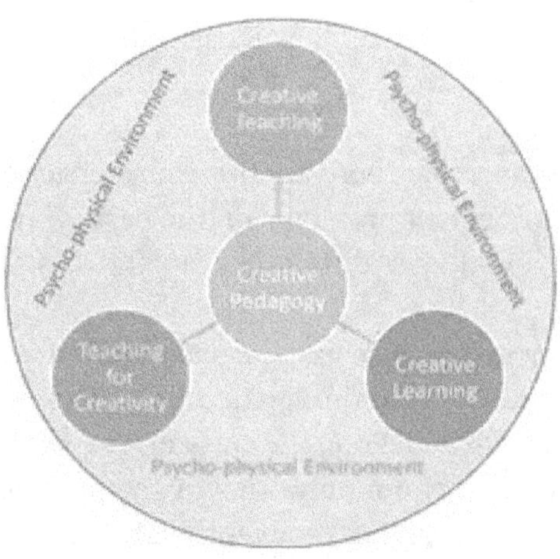

Source: https://www.semanticscholar.org/

Teachers must not only aim to offer releasers but also to remove blockages to encourage creativity. The recently given conclusions combining resumes like Cropley 19 (1992a) and Torrance (1992) recommend that teachers should provide importance and support to qualities like:

1. Task commitment, tenacity and resolve

2. Independence and non-compliance

3. Trust and willingness to risk being mistaken.

4. Take the lead and tackle tough things willingly.

This might be spoken sooner than done, as teachers typically chew on creative features. Research has revealed that many teachers do not enjoy these features. In the United States (for example, Bachtold, 1974) as well as in other jurisdictions more recent research corroborated earlier Torrance results (1970) in this regard (Howieson, 1984; Obuche, 1986; Raina, 1972). Stone (1980) discovered that two grades pupils with the greatest creative scores had been evaluated as the most commonly troublesome among instructors by their peers. It may be queried how the feedback teachers offer creative pupils if they consider their conduct to be undisciplined, unruly, distrustful or even humiliating. However, there is proof of teachers' support for creativity, overwhelming in the classroom,—Feldhusen and Treffinger (1975) claim that 96% of instructors have taken this position. The issue seems to be the recognition of 'immature' creative potential versus the recognition of creative potential; definitely, many teachers are often confronted by really disruptive behavior. Again, the problem of identifying and separating signs of creative potential from misconduct is highlighted here. 20 In this respect, an intriguing result is that creative professors prefer to provide creative pupils greater assistance. Milgram (1979) showed that instructor creativity and student creativity correlated. McLeod and Cropley (1989) referred to professors who look particularly comfortable with creative pupils as "creativity nurturing." As Cropley (1982) has pointed out, these teachers provide a model of creative behaviour, strengthen such behavior, while students demonstrate it, protect creative students against pressure of conformity from their peers, provide safe refuge for their students, when they are ridiculed and criticized by other peers, parents or professors. Cropley (1982) reports that people that promote creativity are the teachers:

1 Encourage students to learn independently

2 Have a cooperative, socially integrated teaching approach

3 Ensure that their pupils have a good basis for diverse thinking.

4 Facilitatc flexible thinking in students

5 Foster self-assessment in students

6 Take student suggestions and questions seriously

7 Offer student's opportunities to work with various materials and under a variety of different conditions.

8 Deliver the students' ideas until they are carefully developed and clearly formulated

9 Help pupils get the confidence to try out new and odd things to cope with frustration and frailty.

Creativity and Innovation Models

Imagination and development cooperate to make an answer for an issue or carry another experience to society. The accompanying rundown Here are seven imaginative developments:

Ride hailing

The presentation of ride hailing created another vehicle-for-employ transportation administration that was at first constrained by cabs. The main organization to offer this assistance imagination conceptualized ride hailing and project worker based individual driving frameworks to create adaptable work open doors and vehicle for employ access speedier and more reasonable. The underlying development worked with the making of comparable administrations by different organizations.

Vehicles

Before the vehicle, there were horse-drawn carriages, trollies and trains. The innovators of the auto saw a requirement for quicker customized transportation. The car everlastingly altered the manner in which individuals travel. The development of the main vehicle filled ensuing advancements.

Chiaroscuro

In workmanship, chiaroscuro is a strategy for articulation utilizing sharp differentiations among dimness and light to make a one of a kind environment and creation. The individual who made this thought needed to design an innovative strategy for delivering more reasonable symbolism and a feeling of three-layered volume. In this vein, their imagination lead to a real procedure that different craftsmen could use to create something similar or comparable impact.

Web indexes

Web indexes are one of the most notable instances of contemporary advancement. Because of the conceptualization of a space that offers a lot more extensive web-based insight for buyers, web indexes became one of the main devices of innovative and web data procurement. Web search tools capability as information base pursuit frameworks, smoothing out the limit with regards to human learning.

Cellphones

The worldwide progress of the cellphone significantly altered the manner in which individuals convey. Before the cellphone, individuals depended on landlines and different techniques for correspondence. This made correspondence not generally promptly open and restricted somebody to a particular area if they had any desire to converse with others. The makers of the cellphone saw a requirement for versatile correspondence and conceptualized the possibility of a telephone that was not restricted to a rope. However the cellphone went through numerous emphasess throughout the long term, it in the end prompted the little versatile gadget that exists today. Cellphones keep on developing from current time advancements and thoughts.

Pianos

The piano is an instrument that developed from the harpsichord somewhere in the range of 1700 and 1720 by an Italian instrument creator. The innovator saw the requirement for a console instrument that could play delicately and boisterously and could support notes on one bunch of keys. Unique instruments of this assortment coming up short on limit with respect to this multitude of highlights.

Erasable pens

Before the erasable pen, pens gave a long-lasting imprint on your composing medium. This implied that an individual unsatisfied with their work needed to utilize whiteout or scratch through what they needed to change. The creator of this item saw a requirement for an answer for this issue and made a pen that could delete like a pencil.

CONCLUSION

Discusses diversity in evolution and features of creative selection. Selection mechanisms at the level of ideas, individual producers and communities or civilizations are explored. Cognitive selection, interpersonal and sociocultural selection are the factors explored. These variables reflect restrictions on many levels to limit the world's ideational diversity. Problem identification restrictions placed on solution generation by creative persons and limitations. In conclusion, the following topics are stressed:

(1) Creativity is a risky activity;

(2) Creativity is threatened by the adjustment of trade-offs; and

(3) Achieving a balance between opposites is frequently a result of curvilinear relationships between historical and creative factors.

REFRENCES

- Floor, M. A. (1996). Creativity. With Artificial Intelligence (pp. 267-291). Academic press. Academic press.
- Holzmann, M., Schmidt, S., & Unger, F. (2002). How creatives describe creativity: Definitions represent many creativity kinds. Reporters Without Borders, 14(1), 55-67.
- Merchant, D. K. (2018). Defining creativity: do we not have to describe that which is not creative, too? Creative Conduct Journal, 52(1), 80-90.
- Mann, J., & Karlsruhe, M. (2002). Contemporary research on the creative concept: Eastern and Western. Creative Comportement Journal, 36(4), 269-288.
- Builder, G. (2003). What should be measured? A new view on the creative concept. Education Research Journal, 47(3), 235-251 of the Scandinavian Government.
- M. Ben, J. G. J. (1972). The creativeness of the individual who never creates anything fresh and helpful: the notion of creativity as a feature usually distributed. Psychologist of America, 27(8), 717.
- Müller-Wienbergen, F., Müller, S., & Becker, J. (2010). The notion of creativity in the discipline of information systems: past, present and future. Information Systems Association communication, 27(1), 14. Communications.
- Robinson, K. (1982). Extend the creative concept. The Creative Conduct Journal.
- Michel, R. A. (2014). Defining the creativity idea (Twente University, Master's degree).
- Petocz, M., & Reid, A. (2004). The fields of learning and creativity process. Australian Researcher for Education, 31(2), 45-62.
- Karl, J., & Krads, M. (1998). The creative process in puzzles, innovations and designs. Building automation, 7(2-3), 123-138.
- Oh, Oh, J. R. (1980). Thought and creativity primary process. Newsletter on Psychology, 98(1), 144.
- Brown, R. T. Brown, R. (1989). Creativity. In the Creativity Manual (pp. 3-32). Boston, MA, Springer.
- Alice, J., & Karlsruhe, A. (2002). Pathways to map: Encouraging composition creativity. Research on Music Education, 4(2), 245-261.
- Karl, A. J. (1992). More than one way: to promote creativity. Editing of Ablex.
- Handwerk, A. (2006). Encouraging wisdom in creation. Education Journal, 36(3), 337-350 in Cambridge.

- Karl, A. J. (1997). Encouraging classroom creativity: general concepts. 1(84.114), 1-46. The Creative Research Manual.
- Claude, D. Aleppo (2003). Creativity as change and selection: certain key restrictions.